LIFE Never Fails to TEACH

B.T. HIGGINS

Life Never Fails to Teach

Copyright © 2025 by B.T. Higgins All rights reserved.

No part of this publication may be reproduced, stored in a retrieval system, or transmitted in any form or by any means, electronic, mechanical, photocopying, recording, scanning, or otherwise, without the prior written permission of the author.

Although every precaution has been taken in the preparation of this book, the publisher and author assume no responsibility for errors or omissions. Neither is any liability assumed for damages resulting from the use of the information contained herein.

Some names and identifying details of people described in this book have been altered to protect their privacy.

ISBN: 9798349353420

Cover by Olivia Higgins

Edited by Donna Higgins

Images created by ChatGPT and Grok

The Cottonwood Project

3343 Kendall loop Anchorage, AK 99507

Life is the classroom that matters.
Its tests are graded in blood.

Special Thanks
To Donna Higgins for her many hours of work editing and engaging with the ideas in this manuscript.

CONTENTS

Wisdom Mining	9
Language is a Race Car	12
Body Politics	17
Home Run Balls	24
A Theory of Pain Relativity	27
The Demotivation Box	32
The Law of The Scavenger	39
Bad Beef	43
Easy to Spend- Hard to Earn	47
Whack-A-Mole	52
When Ninety-Nine Percent is Not Enough	57
So I Can Be Alive	62
Life Never Fails to Teach	66
Sunday Night Blues	72
Surprised by Product Failure	77
The Pledge	82
Don't Be This Guy!	90
The Fruit Principle	94
When Do You Win the Trophy?	100
Man is Basically Good?	105
Our Dusty Town	114
Don't Hire a Donkey to Paint a Portrait	118
The Bean Smudge Burrito Problem	124
A Gift From the King	130
Hopeless, Sludgy Boredom	135
The Story Our Table Tells	139
"Mustard and Pickle Sandwiches."	144
Do You Panic Or Party?	149

Baby Problems and Super Mommas	153
Bats By The Billions	158
The Silly, The Goofy, And The Gross	162
We're a Flippin' Bottle Flipping Family	166
Where My Heart Finds Its Home	171
My Esophagus Password	176
My Funnel Theory of Clutter	179
I'm Too Embarrassed	184
3D Printed Happiness	188
Helicopter Seeds: Creativity	191
Sugar Addiction: Happy Carb Tuesday	194
You Big Bang Chang	198
Lamborghini: Versace	202
Golden Thumbs Up: Hot Cars	205
The Gutter Tree : Grit	208
What IFs : Game Time	211
Big Hat No Cattle : Big Pencil No Lead	214
Perfection?	216
Perennials: Chronic Pain	221
SpiderMoose: Giant Peanut Butter Cups	224
The Postage Stamp: Bloom If You Dare	227
Drive-By Sniffings : Bagel Voyeurism	230
Other People's Balloons : Insult The Cook	232
Graduation : Bizzaro World Rafting Trip	234
About the Author	236
Also by	237
Follow B.T. Higgins	238

52 Things I Learned This Year

WISDOM MINING

I've spent a lot of time this year ruminating about the meaning of life. Not as a whole because that's not so complicated but the meaning of the little slivers of life. The episodes. The subplots. It has proved to be a much more nuanced challenge. Every day, my life delivers a trial, a joy, a decision, a failure, or a victory. Life doesn't let me peak at its playbook or cheat off its notes, so I am left to my own devices. Why is this happening to me? I demand answers! If today's issues have any rhyme or reason, which I believe they do, no one will help me figure it out. I'm on my own.

When answering the whys and what fors, I suspect most people default to, "Just don't think about it." After all, "Life happens. Just move on." We say we are too busy to mine these moments or it's too hard. Fair points all, but my major criticism for putting my head in the metaphorical sand is if I don't learn from life I am bound to get stuck in negative-decision-loops, like it's Groundhog Day all over again.

That's why I advocate for the second option, which I call Wisdom Mining. It's how I've spent a lot of my couch time during the last forty-seven years. Thinking. Life drops a pile of ore in my path and I shovel it into the old mental rock crusher and see if it contains any gold. Any value. A little wisdom if lady luck should smile. A little personal growth can come from anywhere. Even if the ore piles feel like they are just blocking the way, my inner pirate declares, "There be gold in them thar stones!" Proverbs 16:16 says, "How much better to get wisdom than gold, to get insight rather than silver!" Solomon was pretty smart, I'm told.

I've written over fifty articles about my family, my life, my thoughts, and the fish bowl we are swimming in during the last year. I started this weekly project to provide myself with a creative outlet and preserve my thoughts about the world. A lot of ore piles have been mined. Time and repetition have brought clarity about what I am doing. I've been Wisdom Mining. I've been trying to find personal growth in every trial and frustration, the principle in every decision, the noble paradigm in every anecdote, and the words to live by in every day. It hasn't been as hard as I expected to find the gold. It almost feels like Life Never Fails to Teach. The question is, "Are we paying attention?"

I don't know if my little stories are engaging or relatable to you. Perhaps some of them are mundane, too common for consideration but I think they are important. If wisdom can be mined from my ordinary stories, certainly you have some good ones in your life. Have you been crawling over the top of your ore piles, leaving them unprocessed? Maybe when a big, terrible pile drops on you, nearly crushing your skull in, you get angry and walk around it. If you're leaving the ore unprocessed you're selling yourself short. Not to mention, compound trouble for the future. Who knows what you could do with a habit of Wisdom Mining? How could your life trajectory be changed by a more mature perspective on life? It's a big question mark that can only be answered by digging through a hundred ore piles.

"That sounds like a lot of work!" It is. "I'm too busy to sit on the couch and think." Yep. You probably are, but who controls your schedule? "I'd rather be doing my taxes than process my problems." I get it but Wisdom Mining pays you for your time, unlike taxation, in the form of improved quality of life. "Nothing interesting or important happens to me. It's all just meaningless drivel." Wrong! I have not lived a remarkable life by any standard. If my life is overflowing with teachable moments, so is yours. You just need to create a habit of thinking about it. The good news is you can go back and mine the old piles too. You know, the ones you crawled over and thought would disappear if you just ignored them? Your timeline is full of minable moments and they are all fair game. Choose something, anything really, and start crushing stone. Write it down like I do. Share it with a buddy. Make the goal of working through one pile a week and see what happens. Start a Wisdom Mining club.

There is a great need for these conversations. In the words of the Dread Pirate Roberts, "Life is pain…anyone who tells you differently is selling something." But that's not the whole story. Life is filled with hope, purpose, and joy too. Wisdom Mining has helped me see the silver lining on every cloud, the golden nugget in every struggle, and how understanding helps me grow into a better version of myself.

LANGUAGE IS A RACE CAR

I just finished my teaching responsibilities for this school year. I teach English Language Arts for homeschooled students from fourth grade up to twelfth. At the same time, I completed a college course about language development. The two experiences couldn't have been more different. I discovered that my philosophy of education is vastly mismatched with the standard way that language is studied. Not a complete surprise to be honest as I often find myself well outside the box. The contrast of the last few months has been so stark that I'll need a race car and an elephant to help me explain.

Do you remember that old story about the six blind men trying to understand what an elephant is by touching it? The one who touches the trunk thinks an elephant is like a snake. The one who touches the tail insists it is like a rope. A blind man who feels the elephant's side swears the elephant is like a wall. The story goes on to teach that each man is right to the limit of his experience and yet fails to understand that the elephant is the combination of all its parts. I've noticed that a similar phenomenon occurs as students study language in school but instead of using an elephant to illustrate I prefer to use a race car.

When a student first encounters language studies in school, it is parked alongside all the other subjects in the school day. Math. Science. Lunch. Language Arts. History. Recess. Art. Music and so on. Language arts is a dazzling, yellow race car, a machine built for speed, distance, adrenaline, and sweat but the students can't see that because all the subjects are shrouded by fitted cloth covers. They only know what they're studying because their teacher announces, "It's time for Language Arts, boys and girls! Turn to page one of your grammar books." She dramatically pulls back the car cover to reveal the left side mirror and only the left side mirror. "Today we are going to learn about nouns. Isn't that interesting? Does anyone know what nouns are? That's right Susan, a noun is a person, place, or thing." Then she drops the car cover back down and the lesson is over. The class is left wondering why they should care about language arts but they do know what recess is. Playtime! As soon as Miss Teacher finishes telling them about some guy named Frederick Douglas they can play outside and that's all they're thinking about.

Over thirteen years of language study, they learn all the kinds of rearview mirrors, their names, functions, and rules of use. They know all the other parts of the car too like tires, lights, and something called an odometer. They even learn about a round, grippy thing called a steering wheel but Miss Teacher never peels back the car cover and tells them what all this language stuff is for. As a result, They think language study is about knowing the names of all the parts of a mysterious yellow object. They used to be curious about what the machine could do and who had crafted it, but they don't care about that anymore. "Why do I need to know any of this? I'm never going to use this in real life!" Automatically, Miss Teacher replies, "Boys and girls, stop talking and finish your grammar page."

After thirteen years of language arts class, most kids never get on the road. They don't know what all those parts and pieces are meant to do, and most importantly, they've never strapped themselves into the driver's seat and mashed the pedal to the medal. This is a tragedy. Why do we teach language arts like it's Latin? Language is a race car filled with high-octane gasoline, ready to take us to millions of exciting places. May I suggest we start teaching our kids how to drive?

"Good morning, boys and girls!" Miss Teacher says as she pulls the car cover off the yellow racer, balls it up, and tosses it into the bushes. "This is language arts. This baby can take you almost anywhere you want to go. Hop in, buckle up, and hold on to something." The beautiful, yellow, metal racer screams out of the parking lot onto the highway. Have you seen the movie Ford vs. Ferrari? That's what I'm imagining. Some rubber will be deposited on the pavement. Some traffic laws will be broken. Don't worry. This is a metaphor. No animals were hurt in the making of this sequence.

Miss Teacher screeches to a halt in the middle of the highway. "Better yet, I think you should drive."

She opens her door, narrowly missing a repair truck that is passing by on the left.

"But Miss Teacher, we don't have a license!" She pauses, glances down at the kids, and smiles, "You do now." She pulls a stack of plastic cards out of her pocket, tossing a license at each student like she's dealing poker in Las Vegas. Everyone scrambles to grab their card. Looking down they discover their face on the card in their hands. Below the official logo are the words, license to communicate. They look up with gaping mouths. A stream of traffic whizzes past, horns blaring.

"But we don't know how to drive! We are in the middle of the highway!" The students protest as they buckle themselves into the driver's seat harness.

Miss teacher laughs, and points at the gas pedal. "You can thank me later. Now punch it!"

Language develops on the highway. It's chaotic and wild. There is going to be a lot of crashing and burning. A good teacher will congratulate her students for sheer bravery in the face of failure. "Don't worry about the car, kid. We'll get it fixed up in no time. In the meantime, you can borrow mine." She tosses a set of keys through the air. The students catch them.

"Which car is yours?" The students ask. Miss teacher points. They say, "You drive a rusty, silver minivan?"

"Oh. Yah. She's my baby. Don't let her looks deceive you, she can get anywhere you want to go, just a little slower than your race car. Go ahead! Take her for a spin. Maybe be a little more careful this time, use that brake pedal and rearview mirrors that we talked about."

Once kids get a taste for the places that language arts can

take them, all those parts, pieces, and gauges matter more. They make sense as tools to get somewhere exciting. Once the passion for going places and doing things is lit, the student drives the learning forward. It's a beautiful thing. As a somewhat lazy teacher of language arts, I would much rather ride co-pilot on my student's drive toward success than drag them along like a tow truck pulling a race car perpetually stuck in neutral.

This semester has been very enlightening. I've realized why I teach the way I do. There is a method to the madness and the contrast between my college class and my homeschool class has sharpened my vision for the future. As I go into planning mode for next year, I've got lots of ideas on how to train my drivers. As I push them to become better writers, speakers, listeners, readers, and thinkers, I look forward to seeing them take the wheel with confidence and go farther than they thought they could.

BODY POLITICS

In 2005, Jean-Luc Josuat-Vergès got lost in a series of caves in the French Pyrenees. He had no food for 35 days, surviving by drinking the water that dripped down the cave's wall. When he was found he had lost forty pounds but remained in surprisingly good health and mental condition considering his ordeal. He attributed his survival to possessing a name suitably difficult for Americans to pronounce. Thanks for nothing, high school French class.

A similar ordeal happened to me recently. In a rare alignment of the schedules, I found myself alone in the house for 35 minutes. Without kids or my wife to observe me, and thereby restrain my dieting habit, my willpower crumbled to dust. I proceeded to gorge my way through the pantry. I managed to gain forty pounds before I heard the garage door opening and frantically stuffed all the candy wrappers in the trash. I remained in surprisingly good health considering my ordeal, though my wife noticed the candy wrappers in the trash within five minutes of entering the house. She's like a lady Sherlock Holmes.

The similarities between the two stories are uncanny, don't you think? I mean, they both have the numbers thirty-five and forty in them. Truly astonishing but let's not get bogged down in the details.

I have always found it difficult to maintain a healthy body weight. There was a narrow window in time between my junior year of high school, when I managed to shed the childhood chubbiness, to a few years after my wedding, when I stacked it back on, where I was a lean mean fighting machine. Well, I was lean. Since then, I've been engaged in the battle of the bulge.

Nothing drives home the score so much as photographic evidence. My family discovered my expired passport from high school. When they saw my picture they erupted with shock. My seventeen-year-old son ran up to me. "Dad. We just saw your old passport photo. You were...Wow!" Reading between the lines, I think that means. "You were so good-looking. Very Hollywood. What in the world happened to you?!" I followed him back into the living room and found my entire family bubbling with the discovery, passing around my passport. I took a look and there was no denying it, snacking and time had taken their toll.

I don't mind looking older so much. Time is natural and unavoidable. I don't feel the need to cling to my youth. Age has as many benefits as youth. Not to mention that those who try to buck that system end up looking like plastic surgery zombies. I'd rather be old and crusty than inhuman. But the extra pounds. Ouch! That's my choice, or more accurately thousands of my choices. It's always bugged me.

My problem is too much food. No, that's not it. My problem is I like food too much. Cookies and cream ice cream. Brownies. Candy. Hot french bread. Savory dishes are delicious. Stop that! Don't go down that road. I'm sorry, I can't eat carbs until Tuesday, so I am ultra-susceptible to carbohydrate fixations. Gotta break free of that and rehearse the truth that my body is perfectly fine with the healthy food I've given it. My cravings do not come from need. They grow from want and if you feed want it grows.

My genetics have also provided a "gift." I am large framed... big boned... wide shouldered... husky... strong. You put my family in the Viking age and I bet we would be a powerful warrior clan but in the modern information age where food is plentiful and unhealthy options abound I can pack on the fat in record time. The above story about gaining 40 pounds in 35 minutes is only slightly exaggerated. Of course, I don't know the numbers. I am not dumb enough to step on a scale. That's worse than looking at your high school passport photo.

I've been trying to digest the nutritional advice of the day for years. Deciphering the industrial health complex messaging is like that game where you have to discern which person is telling the lie but instead of five players, you have thousands of influencers and millions of players. What is what? What a pain in the butt! I've tried many diets over the years and do you know what I'm sure of? The weakest link in every diet plan is me. I am the one with a deficit of willpower. Sure one plan may be better than another, I certainly like the one I settled on, but dieting isn't as complicated as it feels. The battle of the chubby hubby is won or lost on any given day in the mind. The problem isn't that you are doing the wrong plan or don't have the right product. It's your will versus your appetites. Simple as that. If you don't start with this fundamental point, it's like trying to explain the existence of Hamlet without Shakespeare. "To be fat, or not to be. That is the question."

With this truth fixed firmly in its place, I have weeded through shelves of rubbish diet books, plans, and products and found a few basic principles to guide my epic quest for leanness. I will share them with you because the one thing this world needs is one more dude spouting his formula for success. Ha! Well, be that as it may, here you go. Commandment one in the Higgins' Dieting Bible: Never pay money for any weight loss program, supplement, treatment, or medicine. You don't need that do-dad or thingy-ma-bob. Pause there for a second. Let that settle. That eliminates most of the clutter and noise in this space. Isn't it nice?

Commandment number two: Since food is plentiful, every time you open your mouth to chew, you give points to your opposition. Therefore, you should reduce the hours per day that you are "allowed" to chew. Intermittent Fasting feels like a fad diet when everyone is talking about it, but it most closely mimics how our bodies were designed to function. Eat when food is available. Fast when food is scarce. And it doesn't violate rule number one because there is nothing to purchase.

In my house, I have to inflict food scarcity onto myself because, though I have been very poor at times, I have never gone hungry. Not once. What a blessing! Thank God for his provision, right?

I started fasting for sixteen hours per day and eating for eight. It took a long time for that to feel easy but one day it no longer required willpower to do it. I had created a baseline habit that I could sustain forever. So I toggled my time to a 7 hours and 45 minutes eating window using alarms on my phone. Then 7 hrs. 30 min. And So on. If it was a little bit of a struggle but manageable, I was on target. If it was easy, it was time to toggle again. It didn't matter how long it took. It became about creating permanent habits bit by bit not being "on a diet." I settled into a lifestyle of a 21-hour fasting period per day and a 3-hour eating window after about two years. By the time I got to that point, it didn't seem like too big of a deal because I had been baby-stepping the whole time.

Had I figured out the path to perpetual leanness? Not so fast. The day came when I realized that the miracle of divine engineering that is the human body and my unique genetic makeup caught up to me. My body had adapted to the new normal and found a way. I began gaining weight again. Are you kidding me? First I got angry, feeling betrayed by my body. After all, I had been doing my part. Though I had not changed a thing, I had found a way to eat my way into the next belt notch in just three hours a day. At first, I did what I had always done in the past when I expanded. Ignored it. Then when I couldn't anymore, I got angry. "This is so unfair!"

The time had come for commandment number three. Carbohydrates are the enemy. Protein and Fat are your friends. Therefore, you must decrease the percentage of carbs and increase proteins and fats. At first, I tried to tackle my third commandment using the toggle method like I'd done with the fasting. Decrease the carbs by small increments but I love my carbs too much. It's like an addiction. No, strike out the word like. It is an addiction. It was time to take some cold turkey medicine. I stacked carnivore or keto or whatever it's called on top of my fasting routine. Six days a week with a Tuesday cheat day. It was so hard. So, so, so, so hard. Addictions are brain battles. I began losing weight again. I thought I had found the magic formula. I eventually settled into the new normal.

Then my body adapted and found a way. Again. FOR CRYING OUT LOUD! I had found a way to eat back all my losses of six days during my Tuesday cheat day. I know, I can see the pattern too but can't I just ignore it for a while?

And so we come to today and the newest toggling of my diet rules. I am currently on day eleven of my thirteen-day challenge. Intermittent Fasting and Carnivore for thirteen days and then a cheat day. It has been hard lately because my willpower feels like an engine running on low-octane gasoline. But baby steps. Two steps forward, one step back is still progress. I give myself grace but never let myself give up completely.

I've accepted that I will look like an old, crusty version of my high school passport but I don't want to be a fat version of it. Honestly, I am afraid that after twenty more years of toggling the strictness of my diet, I will be eating one carrot a day and my body will still find a way to gain weight. I'll keep you posted on that one. Sometimes, I wish God had created us just a little differently. Imagine if our bodies kept our Body Mass Index at the ideal proportion of fat to weight no matter what like it keeps everything else precisely tuned. Now that's the superpower I want. I would be called the Gluttonator. Okay! Okay! I'm done now.

HOME RUN BALLS

Great memories are like the baseball a lucky fan catches off a crucial World Series game homer. Like the home run Kirk Gibson knocked in the iconic 1988 World Series between the Dodgers and the Athletics. According to estimates, that ball could be worth half a million dollars if it surfaced with a well-documented chain of custody. What a trophy that would be. Unfortunately, that ball has never surfaced, and it would be difficult to authenticate if it did.

Well, I caught that ball. Or at least that's how I remember it. I was 186 miles away as the crow flies, but I snatched it right out of the air. My dad was listening to the game on the radio. We couldn't get TV reception at our house because of the mountains and we couldn't afford the cable hook up. So we were enjoying the game like my grandfather would have.

I remember listening to many games being called out on the radio but this one was special. It was the ninth inning.

The game was on the line and my Dad had to pick up my older sister who was finishing a shift a Silver Spur, a summer camp in Tuolumne County. I saw the tension in my father's eyes. He waited for a break in the action and rushed out to the old VW bug we had and tuned the radio to the game. I jumped in the passenger seat.

My Dad zipped out of our driveway, his full attention one hundred and eighty-six miles south. Balls. Strikes. The old-timey sound of radio gameplay mixed with the revving of the little air-cooled engine. My dad navigated the twists and turns of the mountains automatically. He called out to the players. I watched him getting worked up, giggling at the spectacle of my father lost in the magic of the world series. He hooted and cheered when necessary and gripped the steering wheel as Kirk Gibson came up to bat. Bottom of the ninth. Two out. I don't think he saw the road or the cars passing in the opposite lane but he still hit the turn onto the long dirt road called Silver Spur Drive.

The road wound down into a valley. Gibson's count was full. Three balls. Two strikes. This was the same scenario that we played as boys with a bat and ball in the backyard. "Okay. World Series, bottom of the ninth. Full count," and then we would try to rip a homer. Usually, I would miss and have to reset and try again. Now it was happening for real. I kept thinking Gibson would whiff it like I usually did. All that pressure would be too much. The A's would win because of that grand slam by Jose Canseco earlier in the game. Dennis Eckersley, a formidable closer, was slinging from the mound. Then the 3-2 pitch. The sound of the wooden bat on the ball. Clonk!

Vin Scully called the play, "High fly ball into right field, she is gone! ... In a year that has been so improbable, the impossible has happened!" My dad erupted from the driver's seat. He bounced around the VW bug like the last tic tac in the pack. I laughed and hooted and hollered. My dad slammed on the brakes, stopped in the middle of the dirt road, jerked the emergency brake so the car wouldn't roll off the mountain, and jumped out of the car. He danced and jumped circles, pumping his fists in the air. I got out just to watch the show. The roar of the crowd in LA came through the radio. My dad's cheers echoed off the hills.

I later saw the TV clip, which I've linked below. The whole Dodger team rushed the field to cheer Gibson as he came around to touch home plate. They jumped and shoulder-clapped and hugged each other just like my dad and I did on the road to Silver Spur. Yes, I caught that home run ball. The memory lives on forever. Pure joy and elation.

It's funny, the stuff that we remember forever. A father and son sharing a drive. The team's hard-fought battle with an improbable victory. The celebration of the win. Sometimes the unplanned moments are the most magical. The jokes. The games. The shoulder claps. We have made many more memories together since Kirk Gibson walloped that homer but this one is special like catching the home run ball.

https://youtu.be/N4nwMDZYXTI

A THEORY OF PAIN RELATIVITY

The presence of difficulty seems to be inherent to the world. Mankind seems to measure this trouble on a relative pain scale that we have in our heads. The worst we have ever felt is a ten. The lack of any discomfort whatsoever is a one. As a child, you fall off your bike and cut your knee and you think your pain is a ten because you have never felt anything so terrible. Then you contract a nasty influenza and it's worse because it lasts for days. Your internal gauge calibrates for the new worst thing that can happen. You are a kid so we don't realize how little you know.

As you grow, you experience more difficulty of every kind and your misery measurements grow more accurate. You feel heartbreak for the first time. You experience abuse. Rejection. Failure. Loss. Disappointment. You suffer from chronic illness. You break your leg. Your suffering meter measures every event, every tear, every hurt.

One day, you are surprised when something horrible

happens, let's say you cut yourself while slicing an apple and you're gauge only jumps to a five. You've survived worse. This is small suffering in comparison to, and then your mind lists the more terrible things you have felt. This perspective is both encouraging because you can slough off the smaller troubles and unfortunate. After all, the cost of this resilience was too much pain.

On average, this perspective shift comes with your first gray hair. The timing ranges depending on the life you've led, and the pain you've endured. For me, it came during childhood. I would wish suffering on no one, but it does provide a valuable perspective that can not be attained otherwise. Over time, it becomes rare for a new pain to top out your scale, and for new suffering to register a ten. It becomes surprising when the needle hits the red line and all your past pain scores are reshuffled downward.

Then comes the inevitable moment when you start comparing your troubles with others. I call this comparing scars. When I was a boy, my friends and I would tell the story of each of our scars with pride. One story would spur on the next one. "Oh. Yah! Well, look at this gnarly gash on my leg. I got that beauty from a great white shark." I'm joking, of course, but the comparison game is scored that way. The worst suffering wins. But the severity of scars and suffering is relative and hard to compare.

We experience suffering based on what our gauge says not on any objective measure. I'm not saying we can't agree on what constituted bad news, but one man's three and a half is another man's ten. Our brains are the same, our physiology identical but our emotions and perspectives are unique. It's like the saying, "One man's trash is another man's treasure," but with suffering. Gosh, that sounds so morbid.

I've always wondered how my sorrows and trials can feel so huge when, compared to other people and places in the world, I have it so good. I don't live in a war-torn country, under a totalitarian regime, or in a state of extreme poverty. According to my research, a quarter to a third of the world's population falls into these categories, depending on how the calculation is done. Are their suffering meters nailed at a perpetual ten? I can't imagine that level of conflict and trouble.

From the stories I've heard, the extremely poor can be some of the happiest people you'll ever meet. How is this possible? They don't know when they'll be able to eat next, but they don't experience ten-level suffering constantly. This amazes me, but it makes sense. They've seen more, endured more but that only recalibrates their pain settings. I think we all have this in common. Our bodies must find some kind of equilibrium between pain and pleasure, stress and ease. If our circumstances are out of control, we calibrate our perspective so our bodies can exist in the chaos. Conversely, if our circumstances are characterized by peace, plenty, and relative leisure we also calibrate our sensitivity/ perspective so that our bodies exist within the same balance of emotions.

I think we all feel about the same range of pain and pleasure throughout our lives, not because our pain is equal but because our minds make it so regardless of the specifics of our reality. I can think of no better way to explain it. Trouble finds the rich and the poor alike, the free and the enslaved alike, the fed and the hungry the same. We all feel pain, loss, injury, disappointment, desperation, betrayal, and failure in about the same way because our mental machinery is identical. Again, I am not suggesting that all pain is equal, that would be foolish, but all people feel the same range of pain throughout life because their minds make it so. Either by deflating the numbers or inflating them. One to Ten. Pain is relative and our sensitivity to it slowly adapts to our circumstances.

When we are clocking red line ten on our pain-o-meter, we should take a deep breath and think back to all the other worst-ever(s) we have survived. Though this pain is just as real, it is good to rehearse the fact that we have survived pain and can survive this pain too. This too shall pass is not just an insulting platitude, it's a powerful truth. You are not stuck in time, trapped in this moment of horror. You will advance through it as you have done with other troubles. There is no static situation. You are like a train rolling along the tracks. The light at the end of the tunnel is a real thing because no suffering on earth lasts forever. There is hope in that, if you can digest it.

I think it's good to understand how the mind rescores our pain and suffering, allowing us to find emotional equilibrium once again. When we suffer, our minds are learning to take the load. In time we can find peace even if the pain does not subside, and the circumstances do not improve. As a small example, I have had daily back pain for thirty-seven years. The pain level fluctuates depending on the day, so I won't pretend that it's always agony but it has been a big challenge for me.

After all this time, I've learned what can be done to minimize the pain, ergonomics, and trigger avoidance, but most of what I've learned is how to separate the "How I am doing today," from the "How's my back is doing today." That's been a huge victory for me. It is good to remind myself that my pain gauge and my well-being scale are two separate things. My favorite phrase when someone notices my grimaces and asks if I am okay is "Other than the back pain, I'm doing great."

My theory of pain relativity asserts that the mind will calibrate its perception of suffering over time based on what it has felt in the past and what it can handle at the moment. I'm not sure if this brings any immediate comfort to those who are suffering but over time pain relativity brought me back to hope and optimism. Where I thought only darkness existed, I found light.

THE DEMOTIVATION BOX

How many of you can remember playing inside of a refrigerator or washing machine box at some point during your childhood? It's a shame that home appliances don't come in giant boxes anymore. Our last frig came in shrink wrap and a few corner panels, nothing that our kids could turn into a fort. I was disappointed.

I told them about how much fun I had had turning a washing machine box into a secret hideaway. I remember feeling like I was entering a castle when I crawled inside. My voice echoed off the walls strangely as if I had entered a different world—a place with different rules. I could draw on the walls with markers and crayons for one thing. I folded the box tabs part way down to close out the normal world but still allow in light. My imagination ignited. Inside the refrigerator box, the hours flew by. The box morphed from a castle, to a space capsule, to a cavern hidden under an old oak tree where I could hide away.

Then something happened that shattered the illusion and comfort of the box. Someone came along, closed the flaps completely, blocked them, and drummed wildly on the outside. The space transformed into a base drum that I couldn't escape from. I did not like it at all. How had the space shrunk into a torture box of death in an instant? The sound deafened me. I yelled and tried to push the doors open. My chest tightened when I couldn't. What had been a secret hideaway had transformed into a prison. I panicked.

"Stop it!" I shouted and punched the wall hard, bending the cardboard outward. I heard my brother sniggering outside. Come to think of it, it could have been one of my older sisters. My memory is kaleidoscopic on this point, almost as if this same series of events happened many different times. "Let me out!" I demanded.

I pressed against the flaps and they gave way, the light of the world reentered the box. My fear fled away, leaving only embarrassment. I had overreacted and felt silly for it. "Hey, Ben. Don't be mad!" My brother insisted. It had been a harmless prank from the outside of the box, but inside the box, it had felt catastrophic. I crawled out, not wanting to be inside anymore. The fun had been shattered by my claustrophobia. I knew I was being illogical. There had never been any danger and now that my brother had shown up, we could have even more fun inside the box.

But something had changed about the box. It no longer held the same infinite possibilities as a moment before. What had changed? My perspective of the thing. I didn't want anything to do with it. Motivation is a fragile thing for kids, but I suspect all of us. Our emotional reactions dictate how we will view everything. School. Work. Chores. Even games. Only a few elements must shift to create an overreaction like my refrigerator box blow-up.

This memory kept coming back to me. At first, I thought it was because I never forget embarrassing moments. They are burned into the trauma side of my brain. In time, I came to realize it was more than my quirky relationship with social missteps. There was a nugget of gold in the memory that I could mine and it connected to relationships, especially parenting. I suppose my quest to become a better parent is a worthwhile reason to drudge up the past.

In the mind of every person, there is a motivation switch that can toggle on and off. When I could interact with the refrigerator box from a position of freedom, creativity, and curiosity my motivation switch was ON, but what happened when just a few of the elements of the game were changed? I didn't like the game anymore. I became angry, scared, and demotivated. The switch flipped instantaneously. What had I lost? Subtle things like the light, the quiet, my game, and the freedom to leave the box. If I had agreed to the parameters of that game in advance, it wouldn't have been so unsettling. It could have even been fun, but I had not agreed so it toggled my motivation switch off. "Let me out! I don't want to play."

I think there is a simple formula for motivation. Let's use the four walls of the refrigerator box to envision them. Understanding how to switch on children's motivation is very important in parenting, teaching, and relationship building in general.

Imagine a square like the four walls of the refrigerator box.

The formula to create motivation is simple addition, though not every person needs the same amount of each ingredient. Write "Infinite Possibilities" on the first side. This first element is important to attract engagement and relational buy-in. It allows for individual interest to guide and curiosity to lead. In learning, as with relationships, this is crucial. It promises and entices. When I entered the refrigerator box as a boy I first saw a castle, then a spaceship, and finally a secret hideaway. You might have created different possibilities.

We enter into opportunities in our life in the same way a child climbs into a refrigerator box, we are drawn in by what is possible. I think life consists of "refrigerator box" moments, the more infinite the possibilities, the greater the likelihood we will be motivated to enter. Relationships, classes, jobs, endeavors, even a simple conversation is a moment, an opportunity. Will you enter in and discover what is possible or will look elsewhere? I have found that children need some degree of Infinite Possibilities. As mentioned before, some need more than others. The trick is to calibrate the possibilities for age, stage, and personality. Then move on to the second side of the square.

On the second side write, "Easy Resets." When considering refrigerator boxes, a child will want to know, "Can I change my mind?" before entering. If I don't like the first thing I try, if I make a mistake, can I reset? The extent to which making mistakes is not only allowed but easy and encouraged fosters positive risk-taking in a learning environment where outcomes are not guaranteed. Kids are human too after all. No one gets anything perfect on the first try. We are all more motivated to play in a box if we know we can make adjustments as we go along. Put another way, the cost of failure is low and the solution to failure is to learn and try again. Motivation is supercharged when the refrigerator box mimics real life, allowing/requiring second chances, third chances, fourth, and so on.

The third side is "Acceptable Limitations." This is gravity dragging down the tail of the kite, giving it stability in flight. Limitations are everywhere, completely natural. They are guard rails on the side of the road. They are the lines we must color within. Sometimes skill level provides an acceptable limitation. Sometimes knowledge. Sometimes natural talent. Sometimes it's present circumstances. Sometimes it's merely the laws of physics that provide the acceptable limitations.

Life teaches us to live in the tension between our acceptable limitations and the infinite possibilities and whether easy resets are allowed. Wisdom and maturity come as children struggle with these elements and learn what limitations can be pushed back. In many areas they can be, in some the price is too high, and in others it is impossible. The more experience they amass playing in the "refrigerator box" of life, the better they understand which limitations are in which category.

Now comes the all-important fourth side. The often minimized side. The open flaps of the box can be represented like a doorway drawn in architectural plans, an open side. The "freedom" to enter into the experience and the freedom to leave is the crucial fourth element in the motivation equation. The "Door of Choice" can not be neglected without killing motivation.

How do you allow for choice when something is required? You are right. Not everything in life comes with the option of choice, for a plethora of reasons. The point is to create a choice wherever it can be appropriately given. Why? When a child is presented with appropriate levels of choice (age and stage), they learn to make wise choices even when foolish choices are a possibility. I've seen many kids grow up without having mastered this skill. They usually spend their twenties learning the hard way. The key to teaching freedom is to start early and start small.

Fostering an environment of motivation is both an art and a science. You'll have to use your best judgment and calibrate the four elements for each kid, each day. It's a gut thing but don't ignore the data you receive each day. That is how you set the levels for the future. There is no autopilot in parenting or life in general.

I would like to end this article with the recipe for relational disaster. Demotivation is predictable, dangerous, and all too common. Identify it within your default relational settings and do everything you can do, everything, to avoid the pitfalls of demotivating the people in your life. So how do you demotivate a human being?

All you need to do is put them in a refrigerator box of Infinite Expectations, where everything that is done is wrong in some unpredictable way, impose Impossible Resets, where everything that is not done is unforgivable, create Arbitrary Limitations that make no sense, and change without warning, and close the "Door of Choice."

That's all it takes. Now that you know the formulas for motivating and demotivating the human heart, make it your business to cultivate human flourishing in all your relationships.

THE LAW OF THE SCAVENGER

The raven had found something good. It looked like the cone-shaped wrapper of an ice cream, but I couldn't tell for sure. He clutched it in his beak and, though it was bigger than his head, flew to the peak of the roof just outside my window. Without delay, he attacked the inside of the cone. Scraping. Prying. Picking. At first, I thought his vigor came from joy at finding such a bounty in someone's trash. But then, I realized my mistake. It was fear. The rich raven fears losing his feast. The hungry raven fears never finding it.

A second raven landed nearby and made a stab for the food. The first bird lashed out in defense with his beak. The attacker spread his wings and clawed at the defender. Neither bird backed down. They clawed at each other's breasts and beat the other with their wings. With claw and wing engaged in the fight, neither bird could stand. They rolled down the roof's slope like a barrel, their talons locked in battle. Feathers slapped against shingles and I lost track of which bird was which.

I thought they would roll off the edge but one bird surrendered and jumped away just before the gutter line. The victor flew up to the cone and pecked at it. The loser flew away, no doubt back to the garbage can that had yielded such a grand prize. Perhaps something else could be found there before the garbage truck arrived and swallowed it all.

I sat watching the raven on the rooftop, unsure if I had seen a successful defense or a successful piracy. At first, I felt certain the defender had prevailed but the more I considered it there was no way to tell the two large, black birds apart. That left me feeling unsatisfied. How should I feel about what I'd seen? I'd been rooting for the first bird though he may well have stolen the cone in the first place. If possession is nine-tenths of the law, the piece of garbage belonged to him but a quick study of the world reveals the law of the scavenger. "It belongs to whoever can keep it." The only safe food is swallowed food if you are a raven.

I found myself struggling to decide which raven was the good guy and which one had won. My ethical core needed to make a judgment about the Ravens' battle. Why? I often struggle to make the same judgment about geo-political events. Who is the good guy? Which side am I on? Which lens am I filtering the news through? Somehow I automatically transferred this habit to my feathered neighbors. Perhaps that was a mistake in the case of these birds but I can't help it.

Birds live or die by the law of the scavenger, so good and bad are defined according to it. Good is living. Bad is dying. Some refer to this as the survival of the fittest. Some say might makes right. Others use this idea to justify any behavior because it's a dog-eat-dog world. The ends justify the means.

It's all the same basic principle and humanity is riddled with it too, now that I think about it. How are we different from the ravens?

The birds' primary objective justified a rooftop rumble over the bottom bit of an ice cream, despite the risk of injury and what that would do to their chances of survival. Food is life. Only first place gets the trophy. Let the games begin. Why am I saddened when I see creatures fight beak and talon for their next morsel? Why do I have a prejudice for the raven that I first observed with the treat? The law of the scavenger would indicate that only the winner did good. Shouldn't I feel that the winner was right? The loser was wrong? That's often how the history books are written. Great! I was just trying to enjoy the view and now I've got my ethical undies in a knot. It's surprising how often life illustrates and instructs, isn't it?

I've seen dozens of ravens gather around overflowing trash cans after Christmas and Thanksgiving. Ravens are like pigeons in Anchorage during the winter. They are everywhere. They gather where the food is plentiful like landfills, choice dumpsters around town, and certain neighborhoods on trash collection day. There is an air of fear in their behavior because no matter how juicy the garbage only some of the good stuff is accessible, the competition is fierce, and once the garbage truck comes the party is over. It's a fear-based way of life. A scarcity mindset.

I don't want to live that way. I'm not sure why but it also seems unacceptably wrong, as if the world wasn't meant to operate this way but it currently does. I feel, deep in my viscera, that creation was originally made to work differently. "Oh, that's just your Christianity talking." I hear the critics saying, "It'll pass. Just say, six 'Hail Darwins,' and eight 'Our Mother Natures.'"

I can observe that the law of the scavenger is indeed the way of the world around me, but I can't cotton to the idea that this is how it should be. We weren't made to live in fear, scraping for scrapes, backstabbing for benefits, and jostling for advantage. The original design of creation was good and God called us very good. That's an A+ mark on our original report card. Then sin. Yah. Then sin came and broke everything. Sin gave us the law of the scavenger. Sin gave us war. Sin gave us hate. Sin gave us scarcity and the fear mindset.

My critics are right to say that it's my Christianity talking. My Judeo-Christian value system is the source of my hope that this world can be better than it is. Without it, I see no genuine hope for this world. The Bible has a lot to say about a better way to live. It urges me to rise above the law of the scavenger even in a sin-broken world. There is a smarter paradigm to embrace, a path to forgiveness, and a plan being executed by the loving creator to fix all that was broken.

It's almost like the ravens are crying out for the redemption of all creation. Let it be. Our loving Father who art in heaven. Let it be.

BAD BEEF

I discovered an old package of beef in the fridge this morning. It had grayed to a color that reminded me it was dead cow flesh and the smell emanating through the bag was suspect. I grimaced at the waste. I saw four dollar bills held over a flame, burning from the left to right across George's face. Somehow it had gotten pushed to the back of a low shelf. When? That was the question I needed to answer. I opened the bag tentatively. I stuck my nose inside and sniffed. It could be a week old or it could be more.

Life is full of big decisions and though I had only been awake for a few minutes another one had been thrust upon me. I upended the bag and let the beef drop into my cast iron skillet. I cut it open with a spatula. The inside of the one-pound lump was bright red still. "That's a good sign." I sniffed again. "Definitely on the borderline."

I cranked the burner on high. "The heat will kill anything that's in there," I told myself. "Most likely." I felt a twist in my gut but began attacking the lump with the sharp edge of my metal spatula to break it down. Soon the sound of sizzling fat filled the kitchen, mixing strangely with the music in my earbuds. I know my Spotify playlist is random, but the soundtrack seemed to be foreshadowing something bad. I wondered what movie the score was from. It had a "turning to the dark side" kind of vibe.

The smell of cooked hamburger rose to my nostrils. A cloying mix of rendering fat and the odor of the ongoing death of a bacterial civilization tickled my nose hairs. I gritted my teeth, considering. "Definitely more than a week." I added Carne Asada to the mix and the smell diminished. Before refrigeration, it would have been normal to add spices to mask the smell of old meat. If they could do it, surely I could.

I bent over and pulled a long draft of air through the nose. Maybe a little more spice. I added some artichoke, jalapeno, and parmesan dip. That stuff could transform ground beef into a culinary circus. A liberal sprinkle of shredded Colby Jack across the top and my meal was ready. I plated it, cleaned the skillet, and left the pan to dry on the residual heat of the burner.

The off-smell was mostly gone or adequately masked. I loaded my fork and hesitated. The bacteria surely couldn't have survived the inferno I'd just put it through. Las Vegas odds makers marked the chances of my regretting this decision at 1 to 3. I took a bite. Moved it around over my tongue. I could tell the cheese and spice were working hard but the taste was non-optimal. Maybe my chances were more like thirty-five percent that everything would be fine. Thirty-five to forty. Somewhere in there. The smart money still said I would be fine.

I chewed and considered my life. What a privilege to live in the age of refrigeration where this conundrum of mine was a mistake rather than an unavoidable reality. My gut clenched and I decided that this meat bowl, so perfectly browned and seasoned, just wasn't worth the risk. I spit it out and watched my masticated blob splatter across the top of my still-pipping hot plate. That would be about five dollars wasted now. That means I just torched a Lincoln.

The sunk cost fallacy began to work its manipulation on my mind. How could I waste all this? The chunk of chewed beef on top of my dish dissuaded me. What a privilege to have enough buffer in my monthly budget that I don't have to face the choice of risking this questionable cuisine or going hungry. Around the world today or compared with all of human history, I am a very rich man to be able to throw away four dollars worth of meat. What a blessing.

I scraped the risky business into the trash and hoped my wife didn't see it or I would have to justify my choice to her satisfaction. In the fridge, I found the bag of 80/20 ground beef I had intended to cook for my morning burger steak before I discovered the overaged package behind the eggs. I cranked the dial on the gas stove. Click. Click. Click. A puff of blue flame lit the underside of my cast iron. I pressed the beef thin so it would cook through just as a nice scald developed on each side. I lay down a crown of Parmesan flakes and shredded cheese.

As I wrote this article, I devoured my delicious burger steak. My stomach filled to the point of contentment, not more. My stomach is doubly thankful that there will be no risk of food poisoning-induced nausea. Though, I still do wonder if I would have gotten sick. Ah, the paths not taken in life... you know what I mean? They could be SO MUCH WORSE. Another blessing.

How did I get into this enviable place in life where I have the financial buffer to not eat bad beef just because I am risk-averse? The countless small budgeting decisions my wife and I made over the past twenty-five years led to my current station. That line reads like a joke because we don't have a high station but it's still true. All the things we did and didn't do created our current stable circumstances. Everything I do today, financially and otherwise, will create the walls and fences of my financial freedom or slavery tomorrow.

While most of the people who read this take the choice to reject bad beef for granted, we would be wise to pause and thank God for our daily bread and good burger steaks because there are less fortunate people everywhere who would love to be were you are in life.

EASY TO SPEND - HARD TO EARN

I find myself browsing through an unending array of tactical tomahawks on Amazon. Some are designed for throwing, others for woodcraft, and others are meant to look mean. I believe the technical term for that look is TACTICOOL. I don't know why I want one, but I do. Cold Steel War Hawk with Sheath. USMC Tactical Tomahawk. 17.5 inch Full Tang Camping Axe Tomahawk with Nylon Sheath. Ridge Runner 18-inch Tactical Axe with Multi-Tool Hammer in the color blue! The images flicker across my screen.

Do I need a tomahawk or even a camp axe? No, I do not. We already have a serviceable camp axe. We use it during the summer to chop kindling for the campfire. Occasionally. It isn't "tacticool" though. It's just practical. If I got the tomahawk, I could mount it on the wall by my bed and, I don't know, look at it. It looks manly. Don't guys need manly stuff like this?

I move the USMC Tactical to my "save for later" list. The

picture stares back at me as if it is disappointed in my life choices. It wants to live on my bedroom wall and help me feel like a tougher dude. I consider the picture, imagine myself brandishing it in front of the mirror-like The Last of the Mohicans, and put it back in my cart. My finger hovers over the buy button. It has free shipping. It's on sale. The description says, "Whether you're a Marine or simply need a reliable tool for outdoor adventures, the USMC Tactical Tomahawk delivers in every way." What! Did you hear that? It delivers in every way!

I glance up from my laptop and notice that my two younger daughters are browsing with Mom on Amazon too. They are scrolling through Barbie Dolls and accessories. I hear them "Ooo" ing and "Ah" ing. I watch as the Barbie Careers Play Set appears in our Amazon cart on my laptop. Then the Style Shine 50 Pack Doll Clothes and Accessories. The Barbie Dreamtopia Chelsea Mermaid Doll with Coral-Colored Hair and Tail. I hear them making giddy sounds of joy and realize that's what my thoughts would sound like if I'd voiced them. I pause and look around the room. There is a newly arrived package nearby.

My Son received his order today. The box is strewn across his desk. It's the most tacticool "Nerf" gun I've ever seen. The Worker Seagull CQB Blaster. I didn't know they made grown-up versions of the Nerf gun concept. This baby spits foam bullets up to a scorching two hundred and twenty-nine feet per second depending on spring weight and barrel length, which can be customized. Wait, did I read that graph right? I can testify that they really sting when they strike, let's say, the back of your leg!

My boy drapes a blanket across the hall, cuts six holes in the shipping box to use as bull's eyes, and starts target shooting. Thwap! Thwap! The house echoes with the sound of the impacts. It's accurate. It's hard-hitting. "Everyone will line up to get in on the action." The gun is awesome. I'm pretty sure his entire circle of friends will have one soon.

My oldest daughter is into camera gear and customized merch from famous movie franchises. The former is a business expense. The latter is a style statement. I see several of her items in the Amazon "save for later" list. My wife? Sometimes, I think she loves toys more than the kids. She loves cute small stuff like Calico Critters, Mini Brands, and Lego sets of all kinds. It's not uncommon to see her constructing a complicated Lego set in the evening like Lord Business from the LEGO MOVIE.

I look back at the tactical tomahawk in my cart and pause. When did we all get sucked into toy shopping online? On one hand, I think it's amazing that we can order almost any product in the world while sitting on the couch in our pajamas in the middle of Alaska. We live so far from where any of it is made and yet in a week or four (Alaska does not enjoy quick shipping times) it can be on our doorstep. The smile-shaped arrow on the brown box seems to hint that we made the right choice. It's a real miracle of modern life if you stop to think about it. Everything in our house came from somewhere else, from the bananas to the vacuum cleaner, to the frog aquarium. It's a gift but there is a downside.

All the friction of buying things has been removed. Wait! That sounds like it's a good thing. It's not. In the old days, the friction would make it impossible for me to get a tactical tomahawk. If I could even find one in town, it would be marked up by one hundred percent. Most likely, I would watch The Last of the Mohicans, wish I could be Daniel Day-Lewis wilderness-tough, and that would be the end of it. Without online shopping, I couldn't ogle the tomahawks for an hour and get one sent over with a single click. My finger still hovers over the buy button.

It's an ease of access that used to be available only to the ultra-rich. Thirty years ago, only an extreme excess of dollars could make something like this happen. "I had this lobster flown in from Maine this morning." "Have you tried the Brie? It's imported from France." "Did you know these marble countertops are made of the same stone that Michelangelo used in his sculpture of David? I had it shipped from the Carrara quarries in Tuscany." Those used to be the status boasts of the elite rich, or those trying to imitate the wealthy.

Now, I can get French cheese at Costco, lobster from Maine (if I weren't allergic), and Amazon has Carrara White Marble Tile for my bathroom floor at a price that makes it a splurge but not a status symbol. "Did you know that I had this TactiCOOL Tomahawk shipped all the way from China? Would you like to brandish it in front of the mirror? It makes you look super tough."

We live in a time where the poor and the middle class in the United States can live like the rich of three generations ago in many ways. We have high-tech versions of maids, butlers, chauffeurs, chefs, delivery boys, gardeners, and jesters. I don't think we realize how rich we are. It's amazing. There is a danger in all this access, however. How easy it would be to forget that this isn't normal? In the history of mankind, our convenient way of life was a fantastic dream only achieved by sultans and kings. We should take care not to take our technological good fortune, opportunity, and freedom for granted. "Of course, we can get whatever we want when we want it. What do you think this is, the dark ages?"

More crucially, the blade of easy access cuts both ways. Sure our technology gives the regular Joe the ability to live like the wealthy, but as demonstrated in my families evening of online shopping, it's a seductive thing. A dangerous, slippery slope. "I need a tactical tomahawk for my collection," can function for a normal fellow like "I must have another elephant for my menagerie, Jean-Pierre. Buy it for me and have a servant parade it around the palace grounds during the festival."

In other words, buying for emotional reasons and to impress others will lead the king, the merchant, and me to poverty. We should be careful that ease of access doesn't lead to addictions to buying, clutter, and sick forms of consumeristic worship. A magnetic attraction exists between the human heart and the acquisition of stuff. Let's be on guard against it. The friction of the past used to help us resist and avoid temptation, but now only our willpower can keep the finger from tapping the buy button over and over.

I remove the tomahawk from my shopping cart, close my computer, and get back to enjoying all the physical blessings and provisions that I already possess.

WHACK-A-MOLE

I have tried to move my family out of our townhouse about twenty times in the past twenty-three years. My dream is a homestead in the woods with an internet-based job that utilizes my creativity and need for independence. My wife has her eyes on a mansion in the city. The maid may be optional (if it must be), but a house and lifestyle that is more like our friends is a must.

We've had some difficulty finding any unity on a plan of action. Problem number one is math-related. We are not rich and have little chance of becoming so, but her heart is not swayed. Crazy Theory Alert! I wonder if her extravagant dreams are a side effect of all the princess movies she watched growing up. Disney has been pumping those things out since before we were born. (She will disagree when she reads this. I look forward to hearing her thoughts on the matter.)

I do think that when we tell our girls that they are princesses, we mean metaphorically. It's a good idea to make sure they know they are precious and special, but I think they might inadvertently absorb an expectation of wealth, popularity, and beauty in the process. On one hand, we should encourage our girls to shoot for the stars but when we teach them, "When you wish upon a star...anything your heart desires will come to you," I think we are doing them a disservice.

So back to problem number one. When we research the housing market in our city the price jump from entry-level townhouses to single-family homes in a good neighborhood, in good condition, and with adequate square footage for a family of six is outrageous. Not as bad as other cities, I'm sure, but ridiculous nonetheless. The mansion is not going to happen unless one of my creative endeavors is widely and unexpectedly successful. They are my version of playing the lottery, the odds are about the same.

It's hard for her to accept alternative paths to a bigger home, and for legitimate reasons. We could get a "fixer" but that requires living in a dusty construction site for months or years. Only the flexible, patient, and long-sighted should brave this path. We've been turned off by dozens of fixers over the years. Cinderella may have come from this kind of living standard, but she is destined for the castle, right?

If we settle for slight improvements instead of getting the whole enchilada at once, we could stair-step our way to the castle but that would involve moving many times. With all our stuff that sounds like a reoccurring nightmare. I've got a few of those that wake me up in a cold sweat at two am.

I've researched other states with lower housing costs.

There are so many options. Did you know that there are places where it doesn't snow seven months of the year? What? That's amazing. In some of these more southern locales, we could even afford the big house, but we always balked at the unknowns of a new state, unfamiliar job markets, moving costs, and the fear of change.

Problem two is bigger than the math though. You might have noticed that I alluded to it at the beginning. Our dreams are divergent. Homestead vs. Castle. Rural vs. Urban. Big property vs. big house. If we ever manage to get the math problem fixed we will still be at crossed desires. This has been very difficult for both of us. I feel like I am living in a can of sardines with a neighbor pressing against me on all sides. She battles with the lack of space for six people and all her stuff.

The admonition to "bloom where you are planted," is a hard truth sometimes but it applies to our lives. I think we have built a good family and are in unity about the importance of raising our kids well. We are of one mind on the day-to-day financials so we can work toward stability of provision for today and for our fully gray-haired futures. We both love Jesus and are committed to following His plan for our lives. We have so much to be thankful for. How many couples are at crossed visions on these crucial points? But, and that's a big BUT...we have found it very hard to be content in all circumstances as Paul encourages (Philippians 4:11-13).

I wish I had the answer on how to fix discontentment. It feels like playing the old carnival game, Wack-a-Mole, where you beat down jealous thoughts when they pop up. Practicing intentional thankfulness after you wack each mole is the best strategy that I know but it doesn't seem to keep them down permanently. Give it a week or a day and those thoughts will snap back up. My wife and I have been playing this game for years. We've learned the patterns and the triggers. Practice thankfulness. List it out to slap down jealous thoughts.

I feel that there should be a more permanent solution. If there is, I can't say I've mastered it. I would like to propose a fourth step to the contentment ritual. 1) Identify that the jealousy mole has popped up. 2) Reject the thought process in the moment and refuse to give it playtime in your mind. 3) Practice thankfulness by rehearsing the good things you have going. 4) Surrender your natural expectation to have the things you want when you want them.

I want my homestead and independent lifestyle! It's still on my wish list, but I need to give up my right to have it. I rehearse my step four. "I no longer have the authority to pine for my homestead and independent lifestyle. Feeling resentful when I can't get what I want is now above my pay grade. That's God's business, not mine. I can still work toward my goals, but I have offloaded the mental burden of fretting, worrying, and dreaming about it." Ooo, that's hard medicine. My little rebel heart aches but it is the only way forward. It's the only way to bloom where you are planted.

In the spirit of diplomacy, I won't put my wife's step four into words. She has different dreams to surrender but the process is the same. Identify. Reject. Practice. Surrender. Then, it's a rinse-and-repeat situation I think.

I will let you know if this leads me to the permanent solution I need. Wouldn't that be nice? If it does not, what then? I will keep playing wack-a-mole until God changes my heart.

WHEN NINETY-NINE PERCENT IS NOT ENOUGH

I have learned that there is a vast chasm between ninety-nine percent and perfection. Though it gets harder and harder to improve the closer you get to one hundred, some people are never satisfied. Maybe you are "some people." Please don't be mad at me but this piece is about you.

For these folks, ninety-two constitutes total failure. I don't understand why perfectionists are like this and I doubt they understand it either. They just have to be perfect or they've failed. As a non-perfectionist, I regularly run head-first into the bear trap of their unachievable expectations.

Don't get me wrong. I know that sometimes you have to do one hundred percent of a thing. Like when the daredevil attempts a jump over the Grand Canyon. The first ninety-nine percent of his jump is a complete failure unless he can get the last little bit. It's a binary situation. Success or total failure. If he gets ninety-nine percent of the way across, he falls into a deep canyon like Wiley the Coyote and blows up on impact.

When the international space station is ninety-nine percent sealed against the void, that one percent leak presents a big problem fast, doesn't it? The limited air supply will be vented into the vacuum of space turning the space station into a terrible death trap.

Part of the beauty and challenge of mathematics for me is that it requires this kind of perfection. The equation is either equal or not. It's binary. Success or total failure. Math teaches an important life lesson. Sometimes you have to be perfect or you've got nothing at all. When the situation demands this, we should not delude ourselves into taking performance lightly. But not being a "math person" has also taught me a lesson. We can make an equally lethal mistake on the other side of perfectionism. Yes! Life sometimes demands perfection, but mostly it does not. The immaculate standard is useful for aspiration but is rarely a prerequisite for success.

Let's use driving as an illustration. It can be life or death, can't it? When I am behind the wheel, I try to drive as carefully as possible because I am operating a potentially deadly weapon. If my commercial driving years taught me anything, it was that if I made a mistake, someone could be hurt or killed. Oh…and my job was on the line too, so if I wanted to feed your family, I'd better perform.

I felt the pressure to make one hundred percent safe decisions, but is that even possible? In my experience… no, it's not. Then I must have had lots of accidents, right? No, my safety record is pretty solid. The truth is, that our transportation system is based on a good enough model of safety.

Staying in your lane is not the same as staying perfectly centered in your lane. Making a safe turn is not the same as performing the ideal maneuver. Avoiding the crazies is not the same as foreseeing every move they will make and reacting preemptively. It's not perfect, but if you achieve a safe arrival, no one will be mad at you. That's because we define a successful drive differently than a math equation, a space station leak, or a motorcycle jump over a canyon.

Ninety to ninety-nine percent gets the job done. It might even be lower. Eighty percent or better might be satisfactory. What do you think? How accurate do you need to be to safely complete any given drive? We should look at our life performance the way we look at our driving performance. Good enough is just that, and no one should give you guff about your ninety-two percent. Yet, some people are obsessed with perfection and make themselves miserable trying to achieve it. And they make the rest of us miserable too.

I may be a bit lazy as a rule but I refuse to chase the perfection mirage. I aim for perfection, hit good enough, learn from my mistakes, and count my blessings. Tomorrow is a new game.

Baking cookies is another example if you're feeling peckish. It requires reasonable accuracy, but it doesn't demand perfect measurement. Does it? Ever know someone who assembled the ingredients for a batch of chocolate chip like they were building an atomic bomb? What is the benefit of this kind of approach? The cookies turn out amazing. What are the downsides? Time is wasted. Stress is induced. People are deprioritized. The cookies may be better, but only five to eight percent. Is that really worth it? Not to me. Not to the people the cookies are for. That's a hard message for a perfectionist to hear, but it is true.

That brings me to the most important space where we see perfectionism touch real life. Relationships. How should we handle these supercritical pieces of our lives? Is my relationship with my spouse like assembling a bomb where perfection is required or is it more like whipping up a batch of treats where ninety-two percent works? When I fall short, have I fallen into the canyon and expired in a torrent of flame? Or can I apologize, learn, and try again?

I think it is obvious that relationships are not binary. It's not perfection or failure. I tend to think that perfection isn't required for relationships at all. Relationships require constant attention, intention, and calibration like driving and baking, but you don't need to be perfect. Stop stressing out.

Sometimes, I think we get too obsessed with perfection. We despair. We condemn ourselves. We look down on others for not being perfect like us and therefore disappointing us. We've got to cut that out. I have not been a perfect father, or husband, or son, or brother, or neighbor, or teacher. Maybe I've been eighty-five or ninety percent, but I'm no model of perfection. I'm still aiming high. I'm still trying, but I'm tired of condemning myself for not achieving the immaculate standard.

One of my favorite life slogans is, "Don't let perfect become the enemy of good," and I think it applies here. With relationships, we are dealing with people's hearts and souls.

That means we are carrying precious cargo. But we aren't trying to jump the canyon with all that on our shoulders. That would be foolish. If you think you are supposed to do that, stop. That's not the point of a relationship. Stop trying to be perfect. You are going to hurt yourself and probably the ones you love too. You can't be perfect and you're accomplishing nothing more than stressing everyone out. Oh, and working yourself to death.

No, life is about driving toward healthier destinations, following the map (the Bible), and correcting errors as we notice them. Maybe we don't even have two hands on the wheel and The Beach Boys are playing on the stereo. The whole family might be singing, "Help me Rhonda," or something.

SO I CAN BE ALIVE

Out of the blue, my seven-year-old daughter ran to me and said, "I love you," which would be a sweet gift to any parent. She gave me a warm hug. Then she said something that surprised me. "Thank you for giving in to Mom, so I can be alive. And thanks to God for answering Mom's prayer, so I can be alive." Her eyes were so earnest, her face so serious. It struck me right in my soft, gooey center.

Of course, we had told our younger two daughters how they became a possibility many times, but not recently. I wondered if she had had a conversation with my wife about it. The matter seemed so fresh in her mind. Maybe she was just realizing the significance of it to her life.

After our older two kids were born, I felt I was "at my capacity" for kids. Life was tearing me up and I could not keep adding things. My wife immediately regretted our vasectomy decision and spent five years crying every time she saw a newborn baby. It was really hard for her. I couldn't comprehend, but I'm a man, so that's par for the course. I assumed she would come to accept it with time, but that didn't happen.

Have you ever heard the 1955 Broadway song Whatever Lola Wants? "Whatever Lola wants. Lola gets. There's no exception to the rule." Well, spoiler alert, my wife is not named Lola, but whatever she wants, she gets eventually as well. That is how I found myself going back under the knife, getting the vasectomy reversal surgery. I will not describe that process. You're welcome.

"This counts as your birthday present from me for the rest of our lives," I told my wife before the anesthesia kicked in. The look on her face was pure joy and disbelief that her deep yearning for more kids was now in the realm of the possible. Now that I think about it…why am I still giving my wife birthday presents? How did she manage to arrange that? But back to the point. We have told our younger two that story many times during their lives, but something triggered the memory for my youngest. "Thank you for giving in to Mommy, so I can be alive." That look in her eyes was unforgettable. It got me thinking as I am prone to do. My wife calls them our miracle children. Well. One is the miracle she asked God for. The other is the bonus miracle that God threw in for free. Buy one get one free.

If we are honest, the story of any of our births is a miracle. We are each an unduplicated, unique person. The genetics are fascinating and a bit mind-boggling. Not that I want this article to become about sperm and eggs, but just calculate the math of the lottery each of us had to win to "be alive."

From thirty million to one billion sperm enter the marathon that can, at best, end with only one winner, except with fraternal twins where there are two winners. The unique individual that was you could only be realized by one of those millions. If any other sperm had crossed the finish line first, a different sibling would have been conceived. Not you in appearance, personality, aptitude, or any other genetically determined attribute. Those numbers tax my brain like when I try to understand the breadth of the universe. Stretch.

As I watch my daughters dance around the living room on any given night, smiling and spreading their mayhem, I am struck by how precious they are. How did our family win the personality lottery twice more after I thought we were done? They are one in a billion.

And those are the numbers only on the day of conception, the beginning of life. The contestants would have been different on Tuesday and last month. They wouldn't have been a possibility on any of those days, not in the marathon.

The chances of winning are so small that it begins to feel as if God chose us out of a nation of possibles. I believe He did, though I don't have scientific proof to back that up. I believe he picked each of us for a specific reason, though I don't know what that reason is. You are here, on purpose. Me too. I believe it's true of every individual that has ever lived. The winners of the life lottery.

According to Carl Haub, a demographer from the Population Reference Bureau, the total number of humans that have ever lived is around 117 billion. Seems high to me, but what do I know? Young Earth Creationists, of which I am one, estimate between 50 and 100 billion have ever lived. The shorter timeline is responsible for the number discrepancy. Every one of them was the winner among billions of possible humans.

It makes me thankful to think about the gargantuan numbers behind my wife, my son, my three daughters, and me. Mind-boggling, gray matter stretching, logic surpassing, God-ordained numbers.

LIFE NEVER FAILS TO TEACH

In had just snowed and my back yard, a sharply slanted California hillside, looked like a perfect sledding hill. I imagined starting the perfect sled run at my back deck and winding all the way down to the creek. I would have to find a way to slow down before going into the water, but I wasn't too worried about that. What's the worst that could happen?

For some reason, I never actually answered the question. I was ten years old and invincible. If memory serves, our family didn't own a sled, but I was not the kind of kid to let that get in the way. A cardboard box unfolded into a sheet should do just as well. If I held up the front edge while sliding, I should be zipping down hill like a bobsled team in no time.

I immediately ran into a problem when I mounted my cardboard chariot. The bristly cut weed stalks poked through the two inch snow fall, serving as highly efficient brakes for my sled. Being a problem solver, I deduced that what was needed was a steeper slope to overcome the friction. There was one such place in my neighbors piece of the hill. It was so steep that a small gully had eroded at the base of it. "Perfect. Just what I need," I dragged my cardboard over the property line and staged myself in the best spot. I knelt down, grasped the leading edge of the cardboard and immediately started sliding. For a second, I felt like the smartest boy on earth. You don't need a sled to go sledding. I had outsmarted the system. Isn't that how it always works? You think you have outsmarted the system, just before it eats your lunch.

The angle of the hill directed me straight toward the gully. I realized my mistake, but too late. My brilliant cardboard sled caught on a clump of weeds and stopped. I, however, did not. I flipped headfirst into the gully, striking the back of my neck and then my lower back. The rapid onset of pain was dizzying, but I was fine. I was ten, therefore invincible.

The turn of events had happened so quickly that I struggled to comprehend what had happened. My "sled" landed on top of me in the gully. I couldn't orient myself for some time, I don't know how much time. I remember seeing sparkles of light spinning around in the sky above my head. Trying to understand how my perfect plan had gone wrong, I jumped to my feet and immediately fell over again. How had I not foreseen this possibility? I cried and called for my mom, but I was far from where she could hear me. I rolled onto my hands and knees and stood more slowly. My neck throbbed and my lower back felt bruised. I couldn't see much through my tears but there was nothing to do but walk back to my house and find my mom.

That was the injury that kicked off my chronic back

problems. Not sure how exactly, but during the next week I remember the pain got worse and worse instead of better. Thirty-seven years of back and joint problems later and that moment still seems like the dividing line between my two lives. B.P. (Before Pain) and W.P. (With Pain). The fall didn't create my back problems. The fall wasn't that bad. Nothing broke. I think I had an underlying vulnerability in my connective tissues that the sledding mishap revealed.

But that was that. My childhood ended. Pain causes rapid maturity and that's what happened to me. I had to be grown up now or the pain would swallow me. I went from an innocent ten to a high-mileage thirty in a year.

Life never fails to teach. Pain and adversity are particularly effective instructors. They can either embitter you, or they can make you stronger and wiser. It all depends on what lessons you learn, how your heart responds to the pressure.

Nothing could have prepared me for the severity of the back pain that steamrolled over my life during the next five years. The fifth lumbar vertebra became the fiery source of trouble and resentment, but it somehow made my entire skeleton wonky. Mid back. Neck. Wrist. Jaw. I don't know how, but I suddenly wasn't invincible anymore.

This was a very hard change for a ten year old boy, maybe it would be at any age. I was not prepared for it. Before I could slip, trip, jump and fall without a care in the world. With my new spine I couldn't twist without feeling the fire. Running was out of the question. I became slow moving and cautious because an ergonomic error cost days of spasms. I spent so much time on my back, laying on ice packs, that it felt as if my body had been robbed from me. All that was left was my mind. No, not literally. I am just saying what it felt like at age ten. So, I became a deep thinker.

Sometimes I raged. Sometimes I dreamed. I grieved, battled, and whined. I whined so much that I became sick of hearing myself whine. I prayed for healing. I begged for healing. My thought life became a struggle with God. I realized I had a choice, like a fork in the road. I could blame and reject God because this horrible thing had happened to me or run to him for comfort, encouragement, and strength. I must admit that I wrestled with this choice daily in the following years. Day after day, I would rage and despair. My battle took place between my ears but, in many ways, my entire world had become my mind. It was a gruesome, blood splattered, muddy field on which I fought my emotions as the dragon of pain pursued me relentlessly.

When it became obvious that my back would not heal, I questioned God. When it improved slightly, I thought God had healed me. When the pain flared up again, I doubted and questioned more. I asked why. I screamed why! I demanded that God help me. I begged that he help me. I can tell you one thing for certain, though he did not heal me, God came closer in my pain. He walked with me through my pain. He demonstrated that he was real and loved me in my pain. He helped me understand, in time, that he loved me even though he did not heal me.

My life became a cycle of flare-ups followed by chiropractic visits, massage therapy and physical therapy. This was my new physical life. I could no longer run and rampage through the woods with my brother. I couldn't wrestle. I couldn't...

well, the list of things I could no longer do grew with each re-injury.

It didn't seem like the sledding accident could have caused all of this permanent instability but that was the point where it started. That was my fork in the road. My life before pain. My life with pain. How would I relate to God? That seems to be the main question my back pain asked of me. Run away or run toward. Once I decided to run toward God, I began to harvest the good fruit that can grow from tragedy. Maturity. Empathy. Wisdom and contentment.

My pain changed me, it forged a new person from the ore of my ten-year-old self. It prepared me to survive future crucibles which turned out to be much worse. Without the training ground of my pain, I could not have survived what was to come. Yes, when I say survive, I do mean literally.

When I was a boy, I remember watching a cartoon portrayal of King Solomon's dream. He was a young king making sacrifices to the Lord at the high places of Gibeon. God appeared to Solomon in a dream. "God said, "Ask for whatever you want me to give you"... Solomon answered, "Now, Lord my God, you have made your servant king in place of my father David. But I am only a little child and do not know how to carry out my duties...So give your servant a discerning heart to govern your people and to distinguish between right and wrong." (1 Kings 3:5-14)

I remember being struck by this story and the value of the wisdom that Solomon was given. More valuable than the wealth he accrued during his life time, more precious than a long life, more rare than his fame. Wisdom. That should be the thing I pursue. I prayed, "God, would you give me wisdom too?"

It turns out that God answered that prayer. I've learned so much through my pain. Though at the time, I was probably asking for a miraculous download of wisdom matrix-style. "I know Kung-Fu." What I got was the God of the universe walking with me through pain, teaching me wisdom through every day circumstances. That is an answer to prayer, though it does make me hesitate to pray for the skill of patience or contentment. So far I've learned that life never fails to teach. The questions is what are you learning.

SUNDAY NIGHT BLUES

There was a cycle to the workweek when I was teaching. I pour out my social reserves Monday through Friday, cocoon up to recover during the weekend, and grapple with depression on Sunday evenings. Like the tick-tock of the wall clock, my year was tallied by my weekly battle with the Sunday night blues.

In the first year of teaching, my Sunday evenings felt generally angsty and I couldn't understand why. I am not naturally grumpy or stressed, but something about returning on Monday morning to teaching messed with my mind. I thought that it must be because my first classroom job was hard. I was teaching in LA and the kids ate me alive. When we moved to Alaska and I found a job at one of the best schools in Anchorage, I thought things would be different. I suppose they were in the student behavior sense, but not in terms of the Sunday night blues. Five days in the classroom still drained me dry, the weekends failed to fill me back up, and Sunday night became a darker time. Tick Tock. Time passed.

Slowly, the disassociated stress congealed into a jiggling Jello loaf of dread. At five o'clock on Sunday night, I would fall into the pit of despair.

I didn't want to go back into the box. The classroom. "Don't make me go back in the Boo Box." The old Robin Williams movie, Hook, would come to mind on Sunday evenings. In the film, Captain Hook locks one of his pirates into a chest and drops scorpions in too. They called it the Boo Box. The classroom became my Boo Box, a form of psychological and physical torment that I could not escape from. I began to have strange health problems. Chronic stress wreaks havoc on the body and the mind.

"Now you're just being too negative." People would tell me. "That's your problem. Have you tried looking on the bright side?"

"Gosh! I hadn't thought of that. I'm sure that will do the trick." So I tried to look at the bright side. I liked most of the kids I was around. I enjoyed seeing them succeed. I loved learning. On paper, that should mean I was well suited for the classroom, but no. My personality had a fatal flaw. No matter how much I liked any group of twenty-five individuals when I was stuck in a box with them five days a week, I would be socially drained dry, without fail or exception.

As I read that line back to myself, I thought the dry bucket was the wrong metaphor for what was going on in my soul. A dry bucket can't become drier than dry, but that's not how human beings work. Emotional reserves can become drier than bone dry. Let's think of it like money. I spent all my social capital reserves by Wednesday and went into debt to get to the end of Friday. On Saturday, I tried to repay the debt and stash some cash to spend next week, but that became impossible. I sunk deeper and deeper into the red. My only hope was to survive until summer.

Yes. Beautiful summertime. Eleven weeks to recover, to heal, to repay the debt. In the beginning years, the summer was sufficient to fill me back up. I could go back with social reserves to spend. Each year, my ability to bounce back faded as my resilience dwindled. The cost of each student hour grew. The job began to extract its price from my physical and mental health.

"At least you get a summer break," people would say. "You're lucky."

"Gosh, thanks for that. I feel much better." I began to see the classroom as a battlefield instead of a place of learning. It was my duty to march onto the muddy field and fight the dragons, take my wounds, and get back home to help there. Something was wrong with me. Why was this so hard? I felt like I was being clawed and chewed and stomped by the dragon every single day. I could not win a battle anymore. Something wasn't right. In my defense, I was still a great teacher and my students got the best education I could give, but my soul had to pay the piper. It cracked and crumbled as every day I died a little. I know, the line of emotional death is not as clear-cut as physical death, so some of you might think I'm using hyperbole. When I used strong descriptive language like this at the time, I got looks of confusion or the "come one, man, buck up" look.

I knew that I was in the wrong profession. Beyond a shadow

of a doubt, I knew it. Because of my life circumstances, I was not free to make a change. Oh, how I begged and pleaded. My immovable object lived up to its reputation, so I struggled on.

By the twelfth year, the Sunday night blues involved involuntary muscle tremors and PTSD symptoms. I hesitated to use the soldier's diagnosis at the time because real battle-torn soldiers in our nation were struggling with PTSD and I didn't want to disrespect their traumas, but that's what it was. Post Traumatic Stress Disorder. Except, it was still happening. Nothing I did could pull me out of it anymore. The depression started at Saturday noon and then never lifted.

Finally, I broke. I no longer cared what my immovable object said. I could not continue in the classroom. I found the nearest exit and took it. My question now was would I always be a shell of a man?

The jobs I worked during the next seven years were solitary, so even though they required me to walk through literal dog feces and climb over mountains of refuse, it felt like a field of flowers. No matter how stinky, physically exhausting, boring, or mundane the work became I would shout from the rooftops, "AT LEAST I'M NOT TEACHING."

My weekends became a weekly vacation to whatever fantasy world I was creating in my novels. The dread of going back to work that polluted Sunday evenings was gone. I stopped letting my bucket run dry. If I used a little social reserve, I scheduled as much recovery time as I needed.

My family benefited too because I had some left in the tank to give them. It took around four years for the panic attacks to stop when I found myself in crowds but I still feel nauseous when I have to go into a public school building to vote. I try to avoid driving by the actual buildings where I taught if I can. It's been eleven and half years and I like to think I'm fully recovered now.

I recently dipped my toe into the teaching profession again. Just a toe. I teach one English/Language Arts class per week for homeschooled kids. After a two-hour class, the next day must be a social recovery day. I am finding a balanced way to use my teaching gifts without draining my bucket. Take a little out. Fill it back in right away. It's working. My class is going well. My students are happy. I am keeping it balanced.

When I think about the last twenty-four years of my life and all those Sunday evenings wasted in depression, dread, and panic, I wish I could go back and shake some sense into myself. It has taken as long to heal from the trauma of my social overexposure in teaching, to pay off my emotional indebtedness as it took to accrue in the first place. I can't believe it. That's a lesson in and of itself about choosing your sacrifices wisely. Mostly, I am just thankful to be healthy again.

As I write this article, it is Sunday night. Tomorrow, the new semester of my class will begin. I need to stop jabbering and do some lesson planning, but guess what? I feel fine! By the grace of God, who is in the business of healing our deepest, most baffling, agonizing traumas, I am well again. My Sunday night blues are gone.

SURPRISED BY PRODUCT FAILURE

Do you know that terrifying moment when you realize that you WILL fall backward off the top of a three-step ladder, you will land on cold concrete at best or your head will impact the corner of the garage staircase behind you breaking your neck at worst, and there is nothing you can do to stop it? Yeah, that was Thursday for me.

I am writing this post from a hospital bed where I am currently in an induced coma until my brain swelling reduces to the point where they can...no, no...just joking. It didn't end like that, but it could have. So today, I wanted to talk about how thankful I am for my son. Here is the whole story.

It was Thursday, the second day of January, the first day the Rabbit Creek Rifle Range was open after its month-long holiday in December. I feel like commenting on how annual passes aren't a year-long thing when the government-run facility gets a month's vacation, are they? I will refrain, at this time, from taking that rabbit trail only because I have a near-death experience to relate, and that is much more interesting.

My son and I enjoy target shooting 22s at the gun range when we can, and it finally opened on the second of January. I gathered a couple of revolvers, pistols, a roll of hi-viz target stickers that he got for Christmas, and our hearing protection into a backpack. I slapped the garage door opener and walked outside to start the van. It was single-digit cold outside, judging from the feeling of my nose hairs freezing. The engine started rough, but it started so that was a win.

"You know I would love to shoot the pump-action rifle too," I called back to my son. "It's on the high shelf. Can you get it?"

"I don't see it!" He said. I glanced back and he didn't seem to be trying very hard.

"It's on the top shelf in a box marked Rossi. You should be able to see it."

"Where?"

"It's in plain sight," I felt a pinch of frustration. Why can't he? I started walking into the garage. "It's right up there." I have installed shelving to the ceiling in my garage and it's all full, plus our pantry which fills the space where one car used to be able to park. All full too. I will purposely side-step the "too-much-stuff" rabbit trail as well. I pointed to the uppermost shelf and paused. There was no rifle box with the words Rossi printed on it. I felt a moment of panic and then remembered. "Oh, that's right. I put it in that black case. I forgot about that."

My son seemed to get a bit of satisfaction at my mistake. He may have made a joke to that effect, but I don't recall what he said. I am sure it was something respectful like, "Easy mistake to make, Dad. No problem." I am sure it wasn't anything quippy like, "You're getting a little forgetful in your old age."

"Never mind. I'll get it." I said. I grabbed the three-step ladder from the wall and unfolded it between the chest freezer, the garage stairs, and the wall shelves where my Rossi gallery gun was waiting. I climbed up to the third step and could just reach the rifle bag on the top shelf. We have utilized every inch of vertical space we have in our condo. This is yet another rabbit trail about overly small houses that will not be taken. I pulled the rifle bag down into my arms.

I heard a loud thunk or maybe it was more of a pop-thunk-snap. It's hard to remember. It sounded like metal breaking and plastic twisting at the same time. My left foot lost its grip on the step. I grunted in a dignified sort of way, I'm sure, and looked down. The top step of my ladder had transformed from a perfectly parallel platform to a decidedly non-parallel slide. I was off balance and teetering backward.

Clutching my new rifle which I didn't want to drop, I flinched forward to try to regain my balance without arms and without any footing, which is difficult to pull off unless you're in a Bond film. I kicked at the broken step with my foot, willing it to help me out, but it was no use. All two hundred and thirty-six pounds of me was going down, backward. Hard and fast.

I took a mental inventory of all my life decisions and

relived my most poignant moments. My face froze in shock and a single tear dripped from one eye. There was a flash of bright light and a mournful movie score played as I slowly, inevitably fell backward, probably in super slow motion like when Gollum fell into the lava of Mount Doom in The Lord of the Rings. In reality, I probably grunt-screamed again as I tilted back, back, back.

I knew I would land on concrete or the stairs. The only question in my mind was how badly would I be hurt. Coma or contusion. I waited. Anticipated. Cringed. What came next surprised me. My son caught me. Strangely, it felt a lot like when you drop into one of those giant bean bags. The gentle whoosh as his arms wrapped around me and my back hit his chest softly because he took my weight with his legs. He had transformed into a human shock absorber in an instant. I've always known his brain processing speed was three times faster than mine, but this was like magic. The music in my head changed to a hopeful ballad with African drums and a choir.

He helped me to my feet and we burst into post-traumatic event laughter. I set my rifle on the chest freezer, turned to him, and gave him a bear hug. "You saved me," I said. "My son. Thank you."

"It was nothing, Dad." He shrugged it off as only almost seventeen-year-olds can do. "I just lifted my arms. You weren't even that heavy."

"It wasn't nothing to me!" I said. "That would have been bad, so bad." I shook him by his shoulders and we laughed until the stress bled out of me.

It turns out the weld that held the front left corner of the step to the frame had ripped clean away. Maybe it wasn't the first time I had been surprised by a product failure, but it certainly could have been the last. If not for my son. So here's to raising strong boys who will have your back when you need them most.

THE PLEDGE

I'll admit it. I have issues with the Pledge of Allegiance. After 13 years of k-12 education, putting my hand over my heart and reciting, "I pledge allegiance to the Flag of the United States of America, and to the Republic for which it stands, one Nation under God, indivisible, with liberty and justice for all," I barely heard the words I was saying. It was a school ritual, one drained of meaning like many religious rituals can become when repeated without thought and contemplation.

Have you ever repeated a word over and over, faster and faster until the word starts to dissolve into rhythmic gibberish? Rutabaga. Rutabaga. Try it at your next party. Any word you choose will fall apart along with its meaning and place in the language. The pledge of allegiance became meaningless like an overly repeated rutabaga when I graduated and shipped my carcass off to college. After four years of top-notch indoctrination, I was certified to teach young, skulls full of mush, and, wouldn't you know it, the pledge of allegiance was piped through the loudspeaker every morning in public schools too. Morning announcements and the pledge, and then we were allowed to get to some fine "ejumukatin'."

Many people are offended by the G...O...D part. It's been a full-court press to get any mention of the creator scoured from our schools for decades, and it must really bug them to have the big G front and center in a mandated daily ritual. I love the idea of them having to mumble/choke on those words every day. It must chap their hides. I know I shouldn't get such a kick out of it, but Christians have to wade through so much of their ideological garbage every day that it just seems like the least they can do.

During my teaching years, my principal had such a problem with that line that he spent ten minutes over the loudspeaker trying to get the whole school to say, "One nation, under God," without pausing. All my students were mystified as to why it was so important to him. After all, we all paused on the first line when there wasn't a comma. "I pledge allegiance... to the Flag... of the United States of America." Was there something about the God line that he found objectionable? I think he did more damage to his atheistic agenda by drawing attention to the line than could ever be done by letting the kids chant mindlessly. If I still remember his antics, how many kids do?

We also found that after putting in thousands of repetitions of the pledge with a pause before "under God," it was impossible to say it any other way. By the end of the week, my principal had given up and never mentioned it again.

My problem with the pledge has nothing to do with its "underGodness." Our republic was built on Judeo-Christian principles and no amount of revisionist history can change that. In fact, the line "under God" was added to differentiate our national roots from the communists in the Soviet Union who, by 1954, had built an empire on atheism.

No, my beef with the pledge is more fundamental. Something about a pledge of allegiance to our government rubs me wrong. A pledge is a promise. Allegiance is a commitment of loyalty, which harkens back to the obligation of a vassal to the lord in the feudal system. Why should the citizens of the United States verbalize their subordination to the state? Why do we make our kids do this endlessly? It's contrary to American ideals.

The government has no authority that has not been given to it by its people, and those people retain authority over it at all times through the constitutional system. Why are citizens pledging allegiance to the government at all? It seems backward to me. Since, the government has a subordinate position in our republic all government employees are the vassals of the people, not the other way around.

Perhaps instead of our children pledging allegiance to the government, all government officials should have to put their hands over their hearts and swear a fealty oath each morning. Let every ruler be reminded of their under position in the government/citizen relationship.

When the president is sworn into office, he puts his hand on the Bible and says, "I do solemnly swear (or affirm) that I will faithfully execute the Office of President of the United States, and will to the best of my ability, preserve, protect and defend the Constitution of the United States." So help me

God.

How about every government employee is required to start their day with a similar oath? "I do solemnly swear that I will faithfully execute the Office of Police Officer, or Senator, or Bureaucrat of the United States, and will to the best of my ability, preserve, protect, and defend the Constitution of the United States." So help me God. Let them verbalize EVERY DAY that they are to be subordinate. Let them be reminded each morning that they are responsible for preserving, protecting, and defending the Constitution. Five days a week. Fifty-two weeks a year. It's going to get pretty mundane, but that's okay. We've been dealing with it in the education system for years. They'll survive it.

Their future employment with the government should be based on a performance rubric of these three things before anything else is considered. Preserve the Constitution. Protect the Constitution. Defend the Constitution. Did they do it? Yes. Okay, now are they good at their jobs?

Should students still be required to say the existing pledge of allegiance in schools? No, I think they should not. I think we should institute a different pledge. How about something like this? "I do solemnly swear (or affirm) that I will faithfully execute the Office of CITIZEN of the United States, and will to the best of my ability, preserve, protect, and defend the Constitution of the United States." So help me God. And then we should teach what the constitution says, specifically and often.

The job of a United States Citizen is an important one. More important than most of us realize. We are responsible for steering the ship of state. We are responsible for preserving, protecting, and defending the Constitution. Before any of our employees (government workers) take the oath, we should. If we keep neglecting our responsibility to collectively rule this nation, it will continue to devolve into a common tyranny of some form or variety. Socialist. Communist. Fascist. Oligarchy. Feudalist. It doesn't matter what label is stamped on the package, it won't be the United States of America because it won't be free.

Just in case you forgot what the Constitution actually says the government can't do to us, here is the list:

- Freedom of religion.

- Freedom of speech.

- Freedom of the press.

- Freedom of assembly.

- Right to petition the government for redress of grievances.

- Right to keep and bear arms.

- Freedom from quartering soldiers in private homes without consent in peacetime.

- Protection against unreasonable searches and seizures.

- Requirement for warrants based on probable cause.

- Protection against double jeopardy (being tried twice

for the same offense).

- Protection against self-incrimination.

- Right to due process of law.

- Protection against government taking private property without just compensation (eminent domain).

- Right to a speedy and public trial.

- Right to an impartial jury.

- Right to be informed of criminal charges.

- Right to confront witnesses against oneself.

- Right to compel witnesses to testify on one's behalf.

- Right to legal counsel.

- Right to a jury trial in civil cases exceeding a certain monetary value.

- Protection against excessive bail and fines.

- Protection against cruel and unusual punishment.

- Rights not specifically enumerated in the Constitution are retained by the people (recognition of unenumerated rights).

- Powers not delegated to the federal government nor prohibited to the states are reserved to the states or the people.

- Prohibition of slavery and involuntary servitude, except as punishment for a crime.

- Right to equal protection under the law.

- Right to due process at the state level.

- Citizenship rights (protection against states infringing on national citizenship rights).

- Prohibition of voting discrimination based on race, color, or previous condition of servitude.

- Right to vote regardless of sex.

- Prohibition of poll taxes in federal elections.

- Right to vote for citizens aged 18 and older.

- Right to privacy.

- Right to marry.

- Right to travel freely within the United States.

Maybe, we should have government workers recite this full list along with the oath. It may feel like a waste of time, but when has government made efficient use of anything? After all, how many of their daily schedules would be cleared completely if they followed this list to the letter of the law? Maybe we should start holding them to a stricter standard.

DON'T BE THIS GUY!

A man pushing his shopping cart toward the exit at Costco paused beside the food court table where my family was eating. I saw him through my peripheral vision but paid him no mind. Our Costco is always a sea of bodies and rolling carts. The more people surround me, the less I see any of them. My kids and I were joking, laughing, and scarfing, which had become our tradition after homeschool co-op on Fridays.

"CATHY!" The man shouted at the top of his lungs. I jumped and glanced over at him, startled. It felt like he had shouted directly in my ear. My first thought was one of safety. This man was way too close to my kids if he were drugged up or drunk, but a spot check of his bearing relieved me of that worry. "CATHY!" My ears hurt. The violence in his tone set my teeth on edge.

I followed the direction of his glare and saw maybe a hundred people waiting to pay for groceries. There were dozens of Costco employees ringing up items. They all glanced at the man uncertainly and then immediately looked away. Everyone seemed unsure how to respond to this social violation. I searched for any female in the crowd that knew this guy. Cathy could have been any of them, but I saw no one making eye contact. Perhaps, I should have looked for the women cowering under the fury of this abusive screamer "CATHY!" Was she his wife? What kind of man would speak to his spouse like that in front of a hundred people? If he would do this in front of a crowd, what would he do in the privacy of their home? I felt fear for her.

It sounded like chastising a stray dog for peeing on the carpet. My heart sank for Cathy, where ever she was. It turns out she was across the warehouse. "I NEED YOU TO WATCH THE CART!" The sound slapped my eardrums like the sudden backfire from an old truck. The man pointed sharply toward the food court. He shifted eagerly on his heels. Maybe Cathy didn't understand. Was she trying to mouth the words or sign across the warehouse that their son needed to pee? She did not yell back to him. The man shouted, "CATHY! I CAN'T LEAVE THE CART!"

The son ran through the crowd, his face downturned, and stood by the cart. The man bolted toward the pizza counter. Had the man not eaten for a week? What could justify his rudeness? Did he not realize he could roll the cart into the food court area with him? He'd bothered a hundred people, embarrassed his wife, hurt my ears, and demonstrated his true abusive nature to solve an imaginary problem. What a doofus. I felt embarrassed and ashamed for him. He had no clue what he had done. He was oblivious to the people around him, his young son, and his wife's feelings. It was a blatant violation of the "real man" code. He had perverted his power, becoming a tyrannical lunatic focused only on himself. And for what? A slice of pizza. This "me-before-you" version of masculinity disgusted me to the core.

Whatever his thinking at the time, he resumed a bristly, if quieter, demeanor when he returned to the cart a minute later with a slice in his hand. He had it folded New York style and shoved it in his mouth. His wife and son stood beside the cart and I listened in horror as he blamed his bad behavior on her. Somehow, she was the problem. She had made him do it.

A little bell rang in my head. They have diagnoses for this sort of thing. Narcissists often engage in victim-blaming in situations where they feel criticized or exposed. Deflecting responsibility. Gaslighting. Playing the victim. Shifting the blame. Exaggerating other's faults. He had demonstrated the whole list a few feet from us, in roaring technicolor. The wife, I was horrified to see, cowered under his gaze.

Sometimes the universe provides the perfect example of selfishness, with all its masks dropped, where the naked, gory authenticity of it is laid bare. I turned to my kids as the guy told his wife to push the cart and followed them toward the exit. I waited a second, looking my kids in the eyes. I opened my mouth and fully embraced the teachable moment. The guy would still be within earshot, but that somehow seemed like justice. I said to my kids, "Whatever you do with your lives, don't be like that guy. CATHY!"

It is the job of parents to teach their kids the perils of serving themselves at the expense of others. To this day, I will shout CATHY randomly when I see someone behaving like a little tyrant. I hope they never forget what they saw. I hope I never do either. How easy would it would be to become like him? We all have that level of selfishness brimming inside us. All it takes to become like that guy is a hyper-focus on "me, me, me" at the expense of "you, you, and you."

THE FRUIT PRINCIPLE

Life is full of millions of micro-decisions. Most of the time, I operate on a version of autopilot, making every one of those choices the same way I did yesterday and the day before. There is an order to how I brush my teeth, put on my clothes, and drive to work. How many of you have started driving to work on your day off instead of your real Saturday destination? I've never gotten all the way there but I've taken major detours because of my distraction.

The other day my daughter pounded on the bathroom door while I was in the shower. She shouted through the door, "Dad, can I have my sweet treat yet?" By the time we had discussed whether she had met the criteria for her daily sweet treat, I completely forgot which part of my body I had washed. I had to start over. Strangely, the same thing happened on a different day, but I was toweling off. Whenever my autopilot gets interrupted it takes me a while to remember what I was doing. Then I have to start over to get back into the pattern. Oh…just in case you were wondering, the criteria for my little girls having their "sweet treat" is having eaten their first healthy meal and it is after 12 pm. The rule is meant to avoid daily food debates. I would not call that area of our lives automatic yet, but I'm hopeful.

Most things in my life have become so repetitive that my brain can do them without any new decision-making. I consider this largely to be a good thing as it lets me maximize brain thought hours toward my favorite things: daydreaming, learning, thinking, and creating rather than folding laundry.

On the negative side, this is probably why my life seems to be flying by quicker as I grow older. Most of my life is on autopilot. My birthday is coming up. I had to pull up the calculator app on my phone and subtract my birth year from 2024 to figure out how old I was going to be. I AM lost in my thoughts half the time, but that number seems too big. "The math don't lie!" my phone replied.

Macro decisions are a completely different animal. I use The Fruit Principle to help make these decision easier. Have you ever agonized over a huge life moment? Should you buy the house? Should you marry that person? Should you move? Take the new job? Eat at Taco Bell again? These decisions consume huge amounts of brain power usually for months at a time. For good reason, the consequences are usually pretty high, sometimes irreparable. The Fruit Principle can help.

It comes from Matthew 7:16-20. In it, Jesus says, "You will recognize them by their fruits. Are grapes gathered from thornbushes, or figs from thistles? So, every healthy tree bears good fruit, but the diseased tree bears bad fruit. A healthy tree cannot bear bad fruit, nor can a diseased tree bear good fruit. Every tree that does not bear good fruit is cut down and thrown into the fire. Thus you will recognize them by their fruits." (ESV)

According to Jesus, I can tell the character of a person by the fruit their life produces. Good fruits indicate a good, trustworthy person. Bad fruit should throw up all kinds of red flags. Never ignore the red flags, it will cost you in the end.

For example, if I am considering a partnership with a person, (a business, a friendship, or a marriage are good examples) I should examine their actions. How do they live? How do they treat other people? How do they treat themselves? These fruits indicate what kind of tree they are and are valuable clues as to what you can expect from them in the future. This helps cut through the stress of difficult decisions, especially when the upside seems too dazzling. A good rule of thumb. Never create a partnership with a diseased tree. Never. Never. Never.

This principle saved me from going into business with an angry man who had many common interests with me but whose bad fruit would have poisoned the well of our partnership. Without a doubt, the success of the venture would have been compromised. Getting to NO was a long and difficult decision because the upside of the venture was glistening in front of my face and that can be very distracting. I wanted the deal to happen. Thankfully, I saw the danger of this partnership before signing on the dotted line. I credit this to prayer and God helping me see the red flags.

I haven't always been so lucky. I've made many errors in judgment because I didn't look for the good fruit. I've purchased a lot of thornbushes. Using The Fruit Principle will help you avoid a lot of heartache.

That is why I pre-decide as many things in my life as possible based on my biblical ethics and beliefs. Perhaps you would say that all my thinking time is a luxury you can't afford, but I think everyone should make time for pre-decision. It's free given a little scheduling and prioritization. It might not be natural for you, but it is valuable. Your future self will thank you for getting away from the grind to pre-decide your ethical paradigm.

I spend a lot of time thinking about what I believe and why. In the process, I struggle through scenarios that test my beliefs and the conclusions I come out with are firmer than they would be otherwise. Once tested, every principle might guide a hundred different choices throughout life. It's a major time saver because this process helps me make hard decisions quickly. This allows plenty of margin for the surprises that life keeps giving and the rare dilemma that I haven't pre-decided. I consider it a heartbreak protection device too, but that's just me.

Let's examine a situation where pre-decision could have helped in a stressful moment. I recently watched the first episode of the TV show called Beast Games, in which one thousand contestants competed for five million dollars. It looks like the drama of the show is eliminating people in creative and interesting ways. The first method the show used to whittle down the group was to offer a shared one million dollars to all contestants who would self-eliminate by the time the clock ran out. It turned out that each person who did this won twenty thousand dollars. Not a bad payout because your chances of winning the final payout are so low. Ethically, this decision does not hurt anyone else, so it is an acceptable one you can make unless you just want to go for the big prize.

Later, a different method was employed. Contestants could take a bribe of one hundred thousand to eliminate themselves from the game, but their actions would also remove their row from the game. A basic examination of ethics dictates that the first choice is just fine, but the second is not because you are hurting others for personal gain. Those who took the second choice exchanged one hundred thousand dollars for a list of enemies and a destroyed reputation. For as long as they live, they will be known as the type of person who will backstab to get ahead. Who would trust them ever again? The answer is a fool, in case you were wondering. A good reputation is worth so much more than one hundred thousand dollars. And I mean both monetarily and intrinsically.

This Fruit Principle is echoed in Martin Luther King Jr.'s "I Have a Dream" speech on August 28, 1963. In it, he said, "I have a dream that my four little children will one day live in a nation where they will not be judged by the color of their skin but by the content of their character." This is the way we should judge each other. The "content of your character" rule is the same as "you will know them by their fruits." If humanity were to adopt this as our standard, our world would be perpetually improving, because the only way to get ahead in life would be to demonstrate good fruit. Reputation would be THE currency. Bad fruit would be disadvantaged and thereby disincentivized. Wouldn't that be nice?

There is one further place I would like to extend The Fruit Principle to. Systems. Yes, a person's fruit illuminates the content of a person's character, but the same is true of systems. We can tell the integrity of a system by the kind of fruit it produces. Stafford Beer has a great quote that lends itself well to this conversation. Stafford Beer, inventor of the popular social lubricant (that's a joke), and professor at the Manchester Business School (that's not a joke) coined the phrase "The purpose of a system is what it does." He said, "There is after all no point in claiming that the purpose of a system is to do what it constantly fails to do."

If I had a business called B.T. Higgins' Bicycle Works but it produces jelly donuts, what is the purpose of my business? The claim on the billboard or the product that comes off the machines? The answer is plain, I have a donut factory because that's the fruit I produce. I use a ridiculous example to make my point. In real-life systems, it might seem harder to parse, but so many of them are just as outrageous.

How about a government welfare program that gives money to low-income, single mothers? The sign on the building says, "We are helping the most vulnerable," but the fruit that the factory has produced is a long pattern of generational poverty and a nation-destroying single-parent household epidemic. The need for the program has grown and a permanent poverty class is the result. In a nation that incentivizes single parenting, the government becomes the father and that will undermine our freedoms in the future. The purpose of the program is what it actually does. Its fruit is to disincentivize the one thing that consistently pulls people out of poverty, two committed parents working to give their kids a better financial life than they had. The government will gladly play the role of fathers and mothers, but it would prefer to become your god. I suggest we say, "No. No. And absolutely NO!"

The Fruit Principle as applied to systems can help us make all political, civic, and policy decisions. Filling out the ballot becomes easy. Every election the ballot is chock-full of red flag policies and politicians who are "diseased trees."

We must stop creating partnerships with bad, incompetent, or ill-equipped people and systems. The sign on the door says, "Trust us. We care about you," but the product coming out the back doors is utter and complete garbage."

When we use The Fruit Principle to make big decisions, macro-decisions become as automatic and simple as micro-decisions. The best way to floss my teeth for health and prosperity is one, two, three. The best way to run a nation for health and prosperity is one, two, three. You see? It's as easy as one, two, three.

WHEN DO YOU WIN THE TROPHY?

The homeschool where I teach has end-of-semester and year events called The Genius Fest. Each teacher is supposed to present a few awards to highlight student achievement and celebrate the term. Semester awards are always awkward for me as an English/language arts teacher.

On one hand, it is important to celebrate the accomplishments and work of my students. On the other hand, I have no idea which students will actually utilize the skills that we have practiced and which ones will not. I know which ones behaved well, and the ones that didn't, but every student wrote quality pieces, made brave public presentations, critiqued famous pieces of literature, and helped their classmates improve their work. There was plenty of deep thinking all around.

In my class, we build competence in all five of the language arts. Writing. Reading. Speaking. Listening. And Thinking.

These areas of competence are foundational to our lives, no matter what career we pursue. There is no piece of life in which good communication skills don't improve the situation. We don't know when we will be called on to communicate well, so we need to develop competency in thinking on our feet. Figuring out what we think on a topic and instantly sharing our thoughts in a clear, concise, and confident way is not an easy task. So we practice it all the time.

Any student might have to answer any question at any time. I accept volunteers and volun'TOLDs.' My computer's randomizer program helps gamify this reality. It's loads of fun to watch the tension ripple across the students' faces. If a student has nothing, then we find something for them to say together, and build their rapid development of ideas skills in real time. They always have something to contribute, even if they don't know it yet. Unless they weren't paying attention, and then I just let them squirm a bit. That's kind of fun too. Life is going to catch all of us unprepared or unaware at some point. The best we can do is to learn how to handle the awkward silence with a little grace, a lot of patience, and humor. "Always with humor," is one of my favorite rules.

At The Genius Fest, I have no idea which student should win the trophy. It's too early to tell. The communication game is still ongoing. The language arts all-stars will be the ones who use the experience of standing in from of twenty people, reading their work, and listening to frank reactions on its strengths and weaknesses to grow into stronger people. "I was terrified at first," one student told me, "My heart was beating and my hands were shaking, but I did it and now I know I can. And now I want to share more." Winner. Winner! Chicken dinner! The trophy goes to the growth story, every time.

The cool thing is to think about what that student will do with their new skills in the future. Ooh. That's the big payoff. In homeschool, we are in the business of building up people, not checking off boxes. I love watching students be brave, struggling to communicate well under pressure because they always have something valuable to share with the world. When one of them realizes that their ideas are important, it's time for a trophy.

I'm not sure if the student wins the golden cup for realizing they can do hard things with class, or the trophy goes to the rest of us because we receive the gift of that student's ideas. Maybe it's both. The giver and the recipient win.

During my five minutes on stage at The Genius Fest, I brought a giant, golden cup trophy up on stage. "This trophy is big. It's too big to give out today," I said, clutching the cup in my fist as I gesticulated. "So we'll use it as a metaphor instead." Just between you and me...the great thing about using a trophy as a metaphor is I don't have to buy a new one every time. Hah! My internal business accountant is pleased. Though, I imagine one of my students would love to have it gleaming on their bedside table.

I don't believe in giving out participation trophies and I don't believe in passing them out in the first minute of the game. Life has a long game clock. (hopefully!) I think we should cheer our kids on from the bleachers. "Keep going. You're doing good, but the goal is still ahead of you."

We keep cheering, year after year so they know that we are proud of them, that they can do hard things, and that they have a lot to contribute to the world. The big golden trophy is won when they are living the life they are designed to live, doing the things they are built to do, and helping the people who most need their skill set. We win the big golden cup because we get to watch them change the world and get to say, "I knew them, back in the day!"

MAN IS BASICALLY GOOD?

It is daunting to wrestle with big ideas like the nature of mankind, but that is what we will do today. So buckle up, buttercup! We need to answer the question, "Is mankind basically good?"

Between 1941 and 1945, Hitler's Nazi regime exterminated 6 million Jews, 10 million Soviet civilians and prisoners of war, 2 million Polish civilians, 500,000 Gypsies, 250,000 disabled, 1-2 million political prisoners, and other "unwanteds." That does not include the combined military and civilian casualties of WW2, which rose to 70-85 million.

When I learned about WW2 and the holocaust, it was from a history book. The black-and-white pictures of emaciated Jews at Auschwitz left an imprint, but it was impersonal and blandly summarized in a single chapter of a textbook. It made no more impact on my world than the Battle of Troy. Later I saw Stephen Spielberg's Schindler's List and that film brought it into full, grotesque clarity. I remember thinking something along the lines of, "But it was so long ago, certainly humans have progressed past that kind of barbarism. After all, people always say that humans are fundamentally good."

On April 6, 1994, the Rwandan President's plane was shot down, triggering a violent ethnic conflict for power in Rwanda between the Tutsi minority and Tutu majority. Within hours of the crash, the Tutu started a coordinated campaign of slaughter against the Tutsi and many Tutu who objected to the genocide. Over 100 days, 800,000 Rwandans were killed.

I was in high school when this happened. I remember hearing about the Rwandan genocide. I didn't know the depth of the violence. Hundreds of thousands killed with machetes and clubs would probably be something that is sterilized for the nightly news. Still, I couldn't fathom how humans could slaughter their fellow man so brutally. It seemed like something that belonged in ancient times, not our modern world. It was a demonstration of evil that my young mind had no precedent for.

In my life experience, a school bully was the embodiment of "evil." Yes, I guess I did benefit from a sheltered childhood. I didn't know that some parents beat and abused their kids. I couldn't fathom it. When I learned that my life experience wasn't representative of everyone's, I was shocked, horrified, and confused. How could people do that to each other? I was cured of the naive notion that the mass destruction of innocents only took place in the distant past.

The transatlantic slave trade forcibly transported millions of Africans to the Americas between the 16th and 19th centuries. They were subjected to inhumane conditions, forced labor, and every kind of abuse. This slave trade was finally brought to an end through the abolitionist efforts of William Wilberforce in 1807 and slavery itself was abolished in the British Empire in 1833, three days after his death. The American Civil War (1861-1865) ended the practice of slavery in the United States.

It came as a great shock to my young mind when I learned that that wasn't all of the slavery story. It had existed before, during, and after the history that I knew, all over the globe. It seemed inconceivable. In 2021, it is estimated that 50 million people live in slavery. That's one in every 150 people globally. Slavery isn't a thing we have progressed beyond. The more I consider this, the more I distrust the idea that humanity is progressing at all. If mankind is basically good, as people keep telling me, how are any of these atrocities possible? And how do they keep happening?

As of December 2024, 110 armed conflicts are active worldwide. On average 80,000-238,000 people are killed every year in war. This fluctuates greatly with the number of active conflict zones and the intensity of the wars. It's been like this since Cain killed Abel. The numbers are growing with population increases, but it feels like the same story every generation. I am struggling to see evidence for the notion that mankind is basically good.

It feels necessary to mention one more atrocity, though I wish I didn't need to. Abortion is the modern holocaust, collecting more victims per year than all the wars on earth. It is particularly evil because it turns our most vulnerable, mothers in difficult circumstances, into the Tutu with the machetes. An atrocity that causes lifelong emotional damage.

In 2023, an estimated 1,026,700 abortions took place in the United States. Worldwide the story is even more grim. The World Health Organization estimates that 73 million pregnancies are ended by induced abortion per year around the globe. That's a WW2 level of casualties every year. If we are basically good, how can we find this status quo acceptable?

Okay, that's all I can take on that side of the argument. Though I've only listed a few, I think you get the point. For further evidence of the depravity of man, just pick up a history book. Now we will shift our focus to the light side of human nature and not soon enough. I was getting depressed.

Stories of human goodness are everywhere. They are generally on a smaller scale. One family gives a Thanksgiving turkey to another that is in need. A father and mother love, protect, and educate their children in blessed obscurity. The stranger helps a man who has been beaten and robbed by local thugs like a modern-day Good Samaritan. I believe altruism in any form is an outgrowth of human goodness. It happens billions of times a day. We don't see all of it and the history books could never record all of the good things mankind has done.

Every so often a situation breaks through the news cycle and captures our attention. Remember the kid's soccer team in Thailand that got stuck 2.5 miles inside a cave when a sudden monsoon rain quickly flooded their exit? Watch the documentary called *The Rescue* or the movie called *Thirteen Lives* if you don't remember. It is a gripping tale of humans risking their lives to save the 12 boys and their coach. This story exemplifies altruism in crisis. That's four points for the goodness of mankind. I love it. Doesn't it just warm your heart to hear the good things? It gives me hope.

Some people assert that we help each other solely because it benefits the group's survival. I think that's where the phrase "teamwork makes the dream work" comes from. Sharing resources and banding together for protection. They might be right about that, but does that seem like an argument for the goodness of mankind? To me, it seems like the obvious response to human cruelty as well as the difficulty of general survival. Either way, it is good to see goodness overcoming evil. Everyone loves that story.

Moving on to a common and more mundane form of goodness. I would assert that every honest business transaction is an act of human goodness. We don't usually think of it that way, do we? The business does the work of providing the good or service at a price that the buyer agrees is worth it. This win-win situation occurs billions of times per day around the world, and each one sustains or improves life. That is good. Notice I did say honest business transaction. I know the world has a long history of business interests becoming the rationale for all kinds of violations. Remember, I've read a few history books in my time.

I heard a guy at Best Buy the other day blaming the "Corpo's" for a bad business policy. I wanted to buy an Apple phone without a cell phone plan, but apparently, Apple doesn't allow third-party vendors to do that so I would have to drive across town to the Apple store. The policy was causing me some minor inconvenience, so I wasn't feeling pro-big business at that moment.

He said corporation as a pejorative as if to say "all of them are evil." According to this evil business narrative, businesses do nothing but take advantage of people. That is not the reality. I chose to buy my overpriced phone because I have calculated the cost per hour of usage value and found the price acceptable. That is a good thing. It makes my life better. This basic human interaction is positive and foundational to all civilization.

Sure, when businesses get too powerful they tend to do the same things that governments do when they get too powerful, crush all opposition and steal from the citizenry in any way they can to improve their bottom line. The idea that all Corpo's are evil is also wrong. It's a communist idea. It's the "eat the rich," and "down with the bourgeoisie" for this generation. In my view, the communist ideology doesn't have a legitimate voice in this debate as they have been collectively responsible for around 85 million deaths in the twentieth century alone.

Humans commit everyday acts of kindness, work together to help large groups of people by building charities, demonstrate empathy from infancy, have an innate sense of fairness and justice, and widely cultivate traditions, rituals, and teachings focused on compassion, generosity, and moral behavior. So, how do we square this circle? Is mankind basically good? Or not?

Since we have been talking in generalities, it might be good to look at the individual because that is where all these statistics are derived. Each one of us has the profound ability to choose what we will do, moment by moment. Free will is that glorious and terrifying gift that we are given with life. I think most people over forty would agree that it's easy to mess it up. It takes years to build a good reputation and only a moment to destroy it. If mankind were basically good, it seems to me that it wouldn't be so hard to do good things consistently. It would be my default setting, to give it a computer phraseology.

I don't know about you, but the reality inside my brain is that every morning I wake up wanting to do "my thing." I want what I want, and I want it right now. I don't feel like serving others. It doesn't come naturally to sacrifice my comfort, my convenience, or my agenda for others. It's not even natural to serve those that I love, which makes no sense if I am good by nature as people say.

This is the strongest evidence against the supposition of the innate goodness of mankind. By most measures of goodness, you would probably say I'm a decent guy, but I have intimate access to my thoughts, emotions, and desires. I know that doing good is a force of my will. When I stop trying, it stops happening. This proves to me that I am not naturally a good person. I must choose, minute by minute, whether I will or won't be good.

Okay, so I am naturally selfish. That means that to achieve anything particularly good in my life, I must put my natural appetite to death. That's what Jesus was talking about in Luke 9:23, "Then he said to them all: 'Whoever wants to be my disciple must deny themselves and take up their cross daily and follow me.'" (NIV) The cross for the ancient Romans was an instrument of torture, execution, and intimidation. It was the worst possible death and it was the death that Jesus would die shortly after saying these words. He knew he was walking to a sacrificial death on a cross and he called us to follow him. Ouch! My selfish, little heart cringes.

I think a quick glance through the history of mankind reveals that we have been the instigators of great evils and wonderful goods, but an honest look inward convinces me that mankind is bent and broken. We desire good, we value good, and we aspire to good, but we miss that mark. We pursue our appetite for power and pleasure and rationalize our actions. We tell ourselves that "the ends justify the means," but the ends don't justify the means. They never have. Never will.

The religious tradition that most resonates with my conclusions is the Christian one. According to the Bible, mankind was created perfectly good but since we were also given free will we chose to disobey God and our originally designed good nature was broken. The story of history, and the specific histories recorded in the Bible, are the story of God fixing this fundamental problem.

We are no longer naturally good and we can't make ourselves so. God sent his only son, Jesus Christ, to pay for the debt accrued by humanity's broken choices by doing the most unselfish thing in human history, sacrificing his life for the payment of our sins so that a path might be opened for the broken souls of mankind to be rescued and repaired. Back to the original design.

The original human condition was good. That's why we value goodness, strive for goodness, and are confounded by our inability to achieve goodness. According to the Bible, any human who chooses to follow Jesus has a future and hope. A future like the original plan for humanity. Good.

That takes us to the crux of the argument. Are you basically good? Bad? Neutral? It all hinges on free will and the choice you make.

OUR DUSTY TOWN

There are a lot of ideas swirling around the world, like dust in an old western town. You can't take a breath at the OK corral without getting some grit in your teeth. As you shuffle down the boardwalk past the saloon watch out for that patch of mud. It smells foul for a reason. Oh...and they empty the spittoon right in the road. In this here town, they don't care to clean up after their horses much. If you're not mindful, you're as likely as not to get some of it kicked up on your pant leg. Certainly, the smells will cling to you either way.

The stench in dry times is nothing compared to the intolerable smell when it rains. All the bad ideas congeal into a noxious muck so thick it will pull your boot off. That's why most folks carry a handkerchief around these parts. The smell can get pretty overwhelming. A perfumed kerchief over your nose makes a difference. When you pass the blacksmith's place, watch out. You're stepping crosswise into the prevailing wind. The dust will fill your pockets full of ideas if you loiter in the middle of the road to say, "Good day!"

In my lifetime, the world has become this dusty, desert town where ideas are swirling on every breeze. They fill your pockets, get in your face, and collectively stink up the world. It's become almost impossible to avoid their constant bombardment. Some good. Some bad. Some new. Most are as old as time. Strangely, most of them are pointing to how mankind should live. What choices should we make? How should we treat people? What is right? What is wrong?

It has become necessary, in this modern age, to scrutinize every idea that gets blown into your face to filter the good from the onslaught of bad. I want to discuss some of these concepts as they present themselves because it seems dangerous to ignore them. To passively breathe in every sales pitch that you encounter will, over time, transform you into the sum of everyone else's ideas. You will become whatever your culture is on average or worse. That is a dangerous proposition in a culture deteriorating like our is.

Think about it. Whether you are moral or despicable will be a function of your environment rather than your decision-making. I don't like that idea. It's as passive as a paper boat floating on a stream, the current will inevitably take you down. Sink you. Digest you. Unfortunately, this is a common way to live, but I think it is becoming increasingly perilous to let the modern cultural stream be our destiny.

Bad ideas are easily scattered, shared, and promoted, but they are harder to pick out of your teeth. Let's spend some of our daily allotment of time picking out each idea as it presents itself and avoid swallowing any poppycock or snake oil. How about that for a goal? How about we drill down into the truth and build a foundation from it? Let's build our lives on things that are true, right, noble, and dependable. Sure the dust will still be blown by the wind, but instead of swallowing it thoughtlessly it will flow past without infecting our minds and corrupting our souls.

Perhaps we can drill a well, irrigate a patch of ground, and build a beautiful garden in the Dust Bowl. That's what the timeless stability of truth does. It turns dry particulates into rich soil that can grow good fruit from the desert. Over time it builds richer soil and deeper fertility. Soon orchards and cropland are possible where only sun-baked desolation existed in your life.

When the townsfolk see our little house and garden, they'll see a different way to live. We will become the counter-cultural movement. The radically "new and alternative" lifestyle. We don't eat sand, we grow fruit in it. We cultivate a healthy, deep-rooted life from a sun-cracked wasteland subsistence. Then more townies will start picking the bad ideas out of their teeth and drilling down into the truth, cultivating their own gardens and homesteads. Maybe, we can get together and cut an aqueduct through the mountain to bring fresh water to the dry land. Then what was once desolate can become the most fertile town west of the Mississippi.

Now, consider that. Isn't that a hopeful thought? Green acres as far as the eye can see and any dust that blows is soon captured by moist gardens, orchards, grasslands, and crop rows where it is put to good use by deep and active roots. In a generation, or maybe ten, the dusty old western town becomes a paradise with a legacy built on everlasting truth with provision and peace for today and a brighter promise for the next generation.

DON'T HIRE A DONKEY TO PAINT A PORTRAIT

Creating a cohesive picture from blobs and smears of paint is quite an accomplishment. After watching a few episodes of the show Portrait Artist of the Year, I was astounded by the process—so painstaking, so individual. It's a kind of magic. I myself am a great painter of bedrooms and hallways, though I doubt you would have seen my work. My singular talent is freshening up stodgy, old rooms with new colors.

Then there was my illustrious career as a finger painter in preschool. Even at a young age, I showed promise. I wielded the subtleties of line and hue like an artisan. I tackled the toughest of symmetries with aplomb. In my heyday, none of the other kids could cover a canvas as well. Some might sneer, "peaked a little early though, didn't you?" I don't view it that way. A prodigy is a prodigy is a prodigy. Know what I mean?

But seriously…I do appreciate the mind and craft of the portrait artist. Their tools are so simple, but they manage to represent the world in ways that pictures can not. If you want to reproduce reality, sure any camera phone will suffice. A painter makes judgments about how and what to portray in a subject, making the portrait a special reality. Opinion, emotion, and reality. It connects or fails to land on the heart simultaneously with the eye. Every painting is unique. Every subject is different.

Imagine a scenario where I hired a donkey to paint portraits. Let's call him Jack. What kind of art could I expect? If I laid a canvas in front of Jack, how would he interact with the paints? The hoof is a clumsy tool for a painter. At best, the colors would be spilled, misapplied, and wasted. The process might make an entertaining YouTube video, but not a portrait.

Perhaps I learned from my first attempt, but being committed to my "Jack's Portrait Shop" idea for the county fair I created a series of special shoes that I could fasten to Jack's hoof. On the treads of one shoe might be the rubber outline of a smiley face with the words Jack's Genuine Portraiture. On another, a scary face signed Jack's Genuine Portraiture. Just for variety, how about a sad face, one with cat ears, and one with a pirate's eye patch and beard?

Then I trained Jack to gently dip his new shoe in red paint and stamp it lightly on a canvas. What will I have then? The best state fair booth gimmick in the world!

"Step right up, boys and girls. Have your portrait painted by Jack, the donkey. Only one dollar!" Dip. Stamp. "There you go, kid. One Jack's Genuine Portraiture masterpiece!"

"Hey Mister. That doesn't look like me at all."

"What are talking about kid? Have you gone crazy? Look here. Eyes. Nose. Mouth. Just like you."

"But that's not a--"

"Get out of here kid. Jack is a very busy donkey."

I think Jack's Genuine Portraiture has great potential. T-shirts are an obvious second line of merchandise. Maybe hats? The next step is the Forbes Top 400 Billionaires list.

My illustration is ridiculous intentionally because no one would hire a donkey to paint legitimate portraits. A hoof is a blunt instrument and a donkey's brain, even one as brilliant as Jack's, is incapable of specificity and individualization. A portrait requires the agile mind and skillful dexterity of an artist.

A donkey is moderately good at two things. Stepping on things, (In preindustrial times, Jack would be set to work treading the grain to separate the wheat from the chaff and straw.) and carrying about a hundred pounds of cargo on his back. In our times, wouldn't it be silly to use a donkey to tread the grain when we have harvesters that can do the work so much faster? Why would anyone keep donkeys for beasts of burden when we have invented machines that can do so much more in most situations?

You get the idea. As I look around my world, it seems to me that we have hired a slew of donkeys to paint a lot of portraits. The list of egregious examples is too long to cover here. Maybe, I should write a book called, "Only doofuses let donkey's paint." Strangely, most of the examples involve the government. I wonder why? Let's just focus on one.

Our public education system is so badly designed that we have been stamping out happy, sad, and pirate faces for a hundred years. Maybe a cookie-cutter education was the best we could do at the beginning of the compulsory education era, one hundred and fifty years ago, but technology has progressed to the point where we can individualize every child's education and finally treat each child as a portrait instead of an ink stamp. Maybe we should change some things and start serving our children better.

I know Jack is a lovable donkey, but let's not anthropomorphize the educational donkey. It wastes half the paint and then comes back every year and begs for more paint "for the children." If we are honest, we know that underfunding is not the problem. We can observe that this is true by counting the number of leaching organizations, positions, bureaucracies, and decision-makers that have affixed themselves to the educational donkey in perpetuity to get their little taste. They screech for more funding.

When these people defend the poorly designed status quo, they are looking out for their futures, not the children's. Like a carnival conman using Jack to bilk little kids out of their spending money. Taxpayers are getting scammed every year and students are getting robbed of their futures.

That may seem harsh. Individuals within the educational bureaucracy likely do have good intentions and are offended by my characterization, but the carnival conman is created by the combined effect of all the members of the system working toward self-preservation. System interests win out over what's best for kids. And don't get me started on good intentions. "Good intentions" have paved the way to our current, broken system of education. And don't forget, "The road to hell is paved with good intentions." That's one of my personal favorites.

Maybe we should start designing for efficiency, flexibility, individualization, parent control, rapid error correction, quality, and freedom. I have a feeling that we could make a quality portrait of every child using less paint. The kids wouldn't feel robbed of thirteen years and a future. The taxpayer would get more value for their confiscated bucks, and our world would drastically improve.

Imagine a system where the funding bypasses experts, professionals, and administrators completely so they can not gate keep anymore. The middlemen business is caput. Voters tell elected officials how much to spend. Funding flows directly to individual teachers who operate educational LLCs under the administration of the parents whose kids choose their program. Parents direct funds and decisions for their kids, but no one makes decisions for everyone. One educational choice for one student.

This system would be infinitely customizable, leading to the adoption of best practices for each student at the best possible price. Sounds like a good deal to me. All those experts can open up an LLCs and start competing for students along with the teachers who have been trying to do that all along.

This is the system of the future. Decentralized. Nimble. Child-focused. Cutting edge. Really cool!

If public school paintings are getting worse by the year and low-cost, infinitely customizable, and cheaper alternatives are getting better every year, we would have to be complete idiots to keep hiring donkeys to paint our portraits. Are we really that dumb?

THE BEAN SMUDGE BURRITO PROBLEM

Did you know that when a father lays on the couch to listen to an audiobook like *Basic Economics: A Common Sense Guide to Economics* by Thomas Sowell or a podcast on geopolitics and demography it sends out a dog whistle blast to the best interrupters in the house? I'm serious. Thirty seconds after I hit play, just when I'm getting into the book's flow, my two younger daughters drop whatever they are playing and are magically drawn in my direction. An imperceptible whistle pulls them into the living room. They see me, smile, and attack. I don't blame them, it's the 'dad is relaxing' dog whistle. They can't resist. It's a perplexing problem without a solution.

One or both of them charge like rhinos, slamming into me with bony elbows. (It's not a bad idea to keep a couch pillow handy for protection purposes.) After the initial impact comes the climbing. Their knees dig into leg muscles I didn't realize were sore, toes claw into my stomach fat pinching and stretching it like bread dough, or if I'm unlucky they slip and land on my stomach, full of food.

There is a great Bluey episode called, "Mount Mumanddad" that illustrates this process in animated form, if you are interested. Although, I blame this episode for encouraging my girls to become more terrible dad climbers. It's great fun-for them!

Once they climb Mount Papa Denali, they wedge themselves between my shoulder and the couch. Not to snuggle. Nothing sweet or charming. No, their intentions are far more nefarious. They wedge and push. Wedge more and press harder. Finally, when they can get their legs and arms working against me, they press with all their might. The couch cushions betray me, slipping forward until they can't support my weight. I topple onto the ground. My loud grumbling from the floor only seems to encourage them further because soon they are dropping on top of me.

This morning, after they executed their dastardly plan to remove me from the couch, I rolled myself into a burrito inside our gigantic gray, fuzzy blanket which had fallen with me. They immediately began worming their way into the blanket burrito with me. "We're a bean smudge burrito, Dad."

"That's right," I said. "I am the smudge of beans. You are the sprinkle of cheese and you're the dribble of hot sauce."

I should pause the narrative and explain what a bean smudge burrito is and why my kids mentioned it. It's one of my Taco Bell stories. Here is the nutshell version. I have eaten at Taco Bell maybe fifteen times throughout my adult life. Every year or so, I get a hankering for their value menu bean and cheese burritos. Don't know why? I suspect they spray some kind of chemical in them which must be replenished from time to time. That's a joke, not a conspiracy theory.

I distinctly remember the size and hand feel of a value menu bean burrito when I first had one. Three of them would fill me back in...was it in college? I can't recall so I shouldn't say or my wife will correct me. Over the years, 'shrink'flation has taken its toll on the bean and cheese. It's undeniable. I have the advantage of not eating at Taco Bell very often. It helps me notice the change. Where they used to be cheap but substantial, now they are double the cost and absolutely anorexic.

The last time I went, I selected my bean and cheese on a super-sized iPad menu kiosk because it's become too expensive to hire sixteen-year-olds these days. (Anchorage recently voted to bump the minimum wage up to $13 an hour, so I assume we will be seeing more automation soon. Fewer sixteen-year-olds will have the opportunity to get their first job experience under their belt. The real minimum wage is zero, but don't let me go down a rabbit trail of a rabbit trail.)

I unfolded my bean and cheese to add some hot sauce and saw a tablespoon or two of refried beans smeared across a tortilla with so little cheese that I could count the individual strands. Now, I think this is hilarious and depressing since beans are SO inexpensive, the absolute cheapest you can go, and still get the necessary proteins to sustain life. Beans are Dave Ramsey level broke, "Beans and rice and rice and beans." After re-rolling the tortilla, I held this bean smudge burrito and recalled how it used to be. I would never guess it contained anything if I hadn't just squirted in a packet of hot sauce. It's a tragedy that plays out in grocery stores, restaurants, and family budgets every day.

So, when I got home I told my family the story of the bean smudge burrito and the inflation problem that they were going to have to outsmart when they grew up. We talked about 'shrink'flation too, because that can be even more deceptive. I think it is important that kids know the truth about our economy and who broke it. The rapidly devaluing of our fiat currency is one of my pet peeves. It should be for you too.

Most blame inflation on the wrong people. They blame the restaurant and the grocery store, but a basic economics education reveals the true perpetrators. I explain to my kids about how inflation is pernicious and evil. A hidden tax. An underminer of our society and destroyer of lives. My kids nod as I explain that most people are just trying to survive from year to year. Inflation makes it a lot harder. From the family level to the business level. From the cost of two by fours, to ground beef, to bean smudge burritos.

I tell my children about the leaders, both elected and not, who have implemented and worsened the fiat scam. They are looking at me with blank expressions. Oh, no! They aren't getting it. Maybe they're too young. I lean in to try again. I say, "Over the past hundred years in the United States and in thousands of other places and times strong money has been replaced with weak fiat currency." No. If it's too complicated for most adults to understand how can my kids get it?

"It's the Bean Smudge Burrito Problem," I say in a last attempt to help them see. That, it would seem, it what they remembered because they brought it up again today.

They smile and sing, "We are a bean smudge burrito. Bean smudge. Bean smudge. That's so funny. Tell that story again, Daddy."

It's no laughing matter, but I let it go for now. All my arguments about currency debasers being the greatest villains that nobody knows about in history. How the voters in the United States who tolerated this economic terrorism to be prescribed for their children and grandchildren are to blame. How it will get harder and harder to survive each year, and what that means for their future, all those things melt away.

I remember I am wrapped in a fuzzy, gray blanket with two of my daughters. We are pretending to be a bean smudge burrito and they are laughing. The sound of their joy rings bells in my heart. What a precious gift I have in children who like spending time with me. Isn't that the real treasure in life?

I don't control economic policy. I can't fix the bean smudge burrito problem, but I can love and protect my family well. That I can do. I am confident that we can weather whatever the future brings better if our family is built on a strong foundation. Just like strong money must be built on a firm foundation. Ah. I knew there was some reason for these two disparate ideas to be linked in my head.

A GIFT FROM THE KING

There once was a kingdom with a king who loved to admire his portrait in the hall outside his bedroom. He would enjoy it each morning for one hour before breaking his fast and another hour at bedtime before ordering his bed coverings warmed for him.

As he fell asleep, he missed the warmth and grandeur of his face comforting him, so he had another portrait commissioned by the greatest painter in the kingdom. He had the masterpiece mounted above his bed and rested well under its steady watch every night. After some weeks in which he enjoyed the finest rest of his life, he decided it would be selfish to deprive his people of this same good rest.

He summoned all the painters in the kingdom and set them to work painting. He sacrificed himself for his people, as he needed to sit for hours each day in perfect regal solemnity so the painters could capture his grace.

Soon, the portraits encircled his throne room and hung in the bed chamber of every servant, in the stables, and in the kitchens. Every place with a wall that could hold a nail, a portrait was hung. The words, A GIFT FROM THE KING, were engraved above each image.

The king felt positively magnanimous when he heard how helpful his portraits were in boosting morale among the help, so he hired artisans and painters from all the nearby kingdoms. For efficiency's sake, he sat for dozens of them at a time. Metal workers hammered his face into the shields of each of his soldiers. Carvers captured his handsome glance in post and beam and plaque. These the king sent as gifts to all the nobles and regents of his land. A GIFT FROM THE KING, they all carried the same inscription.

One day the king got very drunk during a feast. A tattooist from a distant land arrived and displayed his handiwork upon the skin of his five assistants. The king demanded, "I will have one too."

"What shall I tattoo upon your skin?" Asked the skin artist.

"Me, of course," The king declared. The tattooist caught the king's wry smile in ink and scar on the king's right shoulder. The king discovered it the next afternoon when he woke from his drunken stupor. He loved it and gave the tattooist a stall in the dungeon so all the lords and ladies could have his portrait drawn into their skin. "Now I will never be parted from the comfort of my image. Neither shall my people."

Of course, tile workers rebuilt the bottom of the king's swimming pool in a mosaic representation of his portrait with a look of merriment. Stylized and abstract though it was, the king adored it and decided everyone in his kingdom should bathe daily from that day forth. He turned positively pruney from the hours he spent looking down through the water.

He gave every painter in the kingdom a cell in his dungeon where they could work in peace. Now that every one of them had memorized his image, the king was freed from the tedium of sitting for portraits from that day on. Of course, since the dungeon had been repurposed for art, the murderers were released. Every one of them seemed rather fond of his image and was reported to leave a flower at the base of his images in the towns and the country on the anniversary of their release. Some noted that they left one flower for each new victim they'd taken since their release. The king loved to see his paintings adorned with blooms on this day. He declared a national holiday. Each man, woman, and child was made to plant a tenth of their crops in flowers which would be cut on the king's day of blooms and placed beneath every image of the king. "See!" The king would say, "I have served the people well and they honor my sacrifice with flowers."

The king sent messengers into all the world that in his kingdom no artist should starve. And so they came by the wagon load every day. The king could not bear to send even one away for how could he deny his people his generous face? They all went to work making art for his kingdom. When the dungeon was full of guests, the king ordered that more cells be built and soon they too were filled. The toll on the king's treasury was great but so fierce was his love for his people, he pressed forward with his project.

The king envisioned a future in which every angle of his

grand visage had been captured in dried paint and hung from a wall. Not just for his servants, but all his people. And perhaps the neighboring kingdoms too. Every peasant would glimpse a view of his regal demeanor before their hands touched the shovel, the kettle, or the plow. The criminally lazy would see his empathy just before their heads were parted from their bodies. A final comforting thought for the condemned. A GIFT FROM THE KING.

Each barmaid would appreciate his glistening green eyes looking on while she poured ale in the tavern for weary travelers. The farmers should see his wise countenance as they plowed their fields and squirrels would hide their winter's nuts in the knotholes of oak trees carved with his smile.

For many years he worked to give himself to his kingdom, one portrait at a time. No matter how tiring and tedious the labor. No matter how high the cost. "All the people will have a gift from the king," he shouted in a moment of fatigue and impatience. " Don't stop. Paint on, or you'll receive my final empathy."

Then one day, after many decades, the coffers ran dry of gold and he had no more food to feed his artists. They starved in his vast dungeons and could paint no more. The king wept for his loss, and he died of a broken heart.

On the news of his death, the kingdom wept and mourned for ten and a half full minutes during which they painted garish, black mustaches on every portrait, plucked them from their walls, and proceeded to burn them in the town square. After an hour, all that remained of the king's memory was the considerable pile of ash, which they spread over their fields for fertilizer. But the joke was on them because the paint the king had commissioned for the prisoners to paint portraits with had contained a diverse array of toxic metals and the number of paintings was so vast that the peasants, finally free of his face, had salted their doom into the land that feed them and shortly died of poisoning. Those who survived went mad.

To this day, no one dares to visit this kingdom for the oak trees are all carved with the portrait of a king with a villainous mustache and all the people are crazy, living stunted short lives. The End.

The moral of the story is…obvious. Don't you think? "Thinking too highly of yourself has deadly consequences."

HOPELESS, SLUDGY BOREDOM

I haven't written for months. No, I don't have writer's block. I still have a river of ideas on tap. But that's the thing about creativity you must turn on the tap. I've been struggling with the "why bother?" I printed out the words BECAUSE IT MATTERS and taped them to my computer to convince myself that it did. It mattered to someone. Somewhere. Not sure why it is so important that my written words be important, but it is.

The problem is obvious, we live in a world where there is a glut of words, all churning and whirling like soapy bubbles in the washing machine. If anything, we have too many words for mine to matter. So my motivational slogan fell flatter every morning when I read it. Soon it just became a taunt, a punch line. My work doesn't matter in the way that I crave, so back to "why bother?"

I haven't lost my love for making things from words. It's magical. It's delightful. It's inexpensive as hobbies go.

Recently, I've been shooting paper targets at the gun range. It's a great way to get outside, but boy is it a money pit. Bonfire is a better word that comes to mind. I shoot 22lr exclusively to try to make the hobby justifiable. Twenty-two cartridges are the cheapest to shoot at 6.5 cents per round (At the time of this writing). Yes, I did open the calculator app on my phone in the ammo aisle to get the cheapest brand. I grew up poor and so that elevated cost awareness has stuck. Every time I pull the trigger at the range, my mind tosses a nickel and two pennies in a jar marked, "gone forever."

Writing is so cheap. It's always been the hobby I defaulted to. Hunting costs more per pound than ground beef. Motorcycles are too dangerous for a dad with young kids and the costs run into the thousands of dollars per year. That's assuming no accidents that bankrupt the family with medical costs. I like gardening too but that's on ice for eight months now and it's not cheaper than buying produce at the store. Not in my shady yard. And the list goes on. Writing is just the best in terms of cost per entertainment hour. FREE. Can't beat it.

But if it doesn't matter, if it isn't making a difference, if you can't see the effects, is it worth doing? Even at zero cost, it's still work. What do I get out of it? Why not just vegetate in front of a screen during my recreational hours? After all, if it's just a hobby, it doesn't matter if I make something or just stew in the video stream on YouTube. Does it?

No one has noticed my writing hiatus except my oldest daughter who elbowed me the other day. "You aren't writing Dad," she reminded. Tsk. Tsk. Am I being a naughty boy when I refuse to write? She's right. I should be writing. It's somehow a violation of my creative self to just check out. I think she gets it. She's another creative. She got that from me, if traits are passed down that way, but she has something I don't have which she most definitely got from my wife. Stick-to-it-iveness. Dogged determination. I envy her that.

It's not that my choice of YouTube videos is not useful. Learning is my other ever-present free hobby, so I've gained a lot of knowledge about a diverse array of topics during my "writing" time. But I can't escape this rising tide of hopeless, sludgy boredom. It's dull and in the background. I ignored it for the first month or so and tried to push it back for month three but it kept rising until it flooded into everything else in my life. Thick, oozy, muddy boredom. It stains everything it touches. It won't come out in the wash. "What's wrong with me?" I keep asking. "Nothing is wrong, but I feel as if something is."

My daughter's words echo back, "You aren't writing Dad." I feel angsty, dissatisfied, and uprooted. What a pain in the boot. Can't I just melt into the anesthesia of screen time like everyone else is doing these days? That brings up something I heard in a YouTube video. Something about how anxiety and depression rates are skyrocketing. How we are all mega-dosing screen time. Maybe our screen addictions have made us all dopamine addicts, jonesing for another hit. Like rats in a maze, hitting the lever to get a little treat all day long. Tap the button. Swipe. Scroll. Dopamine taps on the brain that prevent deeper thought, that medicate the brain so we don't feel the BLAH.

Maybe screens are the cause of our cognitive and mental health decline. So many people are saying they are. We are getting depressed because of these devices and what they are doing to our brains. I tend to agree with them, but my experience these last few months has peeled back another layer of the onion.

What are we NOT doing when we snort hours of screen time? It's not just what we are doing. It's what we are missing. "Oh, come on. That's just you. Don't put your garbage on us," I can hear the non-creatives saying. Though we are radically different in personality, skill sets, and geniuses we all possess a genius of some kind. Shall we call it on the soul level? We are all basically the same.

What are we meant to accomplish with our lives? What thing banishes the hopeless, sludgy boredom for you? It seems to be creativity and writing for me. I can't feel alive and well for long without it. Whether I succeed or not is irrelevant. I have this tendency to imagine improbable levels of success when I write something well. I am a dreamer after all, but I don't need to be a successful writer to be a complete human. And that, I think, is a more appropriate goal. Be a complete human. Screen time blocks our ability to become complete humans. Not only because it is addictive, but because it is a substitute for living a real human life.

And so I return to words as often as I can, because I must. To push the muddy pollutant of apathy away. To feel the pleasure of operating in my gifting. To find contentment in my unremarkable life.

THE STORY OUR TABLE TELLS

I looked over and saw my toddler, wearing only a diaper, standing on a dining room chair with a fork flipped upside down like a murder weapon, stabbing the kitchen table over and over. Thunk! Thunk! Each attack left four neat holes in our pine wood, dining room table. This seemed to be quite rewarding to the little one. I saw wonder in her eyes. In the second it took for me to stop her fork-clutching fist, she stabbed the table a dozen more times. That's forty-eight little holes in neat rows of four. If I had not intervened, I think the table would have been reduced to a pile of chips.

"Don't stab the table, little nugget. You're hurting it," I tried to explain the best I could but I'm not sure she understood the why of the reprimand. My wife and I surveyed the damage. It looked pretty bad, and at the same time, it wasn't too noticeable. The new injuries blended well with the old. Sort of an abused-wood motif that some folks pay extra for these days. Together the dents and scratches told the story of the last twenty years of our family, a veritable diary in the dents. A script in the scratches. A transcript in the trauma. A record in the...yah...you're right now I'm just word riffing for my own gratification. Sorry about that.

Our kitchen table has been through the wringer. Its surface is chipped, dented, stabbed, ink-marked, burned, scrub-worn, and water-weathered. It is four feet in diameter and made of soft wood, so it never really had a chance. Not against our family. Meals, homeschool, crafts, and the toddler stages of four kids. It's seen more spilled milk and hot glue than most tables could dream of. Its lived an adventurous life, you know? I laugh when I see dining rooms with beautiful, show-condition tables. What do they know about what it means to be a table?

I remember when my wife and I bought it. Our table was among the first furnishings in our new townhouse condo and came with matching chairs. The chairs have broken, been fixed, re-broken, and been thrown away long ago. The new ones don't match. They've got a darker stain.

"Is it time to upgrade?" I've asked my wife many times in the last few years. I can see that it is hard for her to have worn-out things. She gravitates toward fancy, clean, and lovely. In pursuit of this idea, I have sat at many Costco display models, sipping a diet soda, snapping pictures, and pricing things out. We've balked at the replacement for a few reasons. The cost of new tables has skyrocketed in the last twenty years. It's a hard pill to swallow. The quality has plummeted too. Instead of solid pine wood, you get particle board with veneer. That's inflation for you. I suppose twenty years before we bought our table we could have gotten an oak wood table for the same price. Don't get me started on the villainy of those who debase currencies. It's a real soapbox for me.

There is also the Matthew 7:6 principle. You know the one about tossing your pearls to the pigs? "If you do, they may trample them under their feet, and turn and tear you to pieces." Translation: does it make sense to have nice furniture at this stage of our lives when the kids are likely to damage it, one way or another? We can always get fancy stuff when we get to the empty-nest stage. Should the table stay or go? We wrestled with the decision.

And then this summer on a particularly sunny day, I opted for option C. Give the old girl a facelift, or to put it more diplomatically, upcycle the kitchen table. I disassembled it, took the pieces outside, and began sanding. I had no idea things would get so messy. Sawdust flew everywhere. (Pro tip: Always remember to close the garage door when belt sanding your kitchen table. That is unless you want all your wife's stuff covered in dust. Oops! We'll save that life lesson for another time.)

Chipped lacquer disappeared under the relentless fury of 80 grit sandpaper, and the stab holes too. That razor knife scratch vanished quickly. The laser cutter burn took some doing, but I managed to erase that mistake from the record as well. Do you know what I discovered? Underneath all that surface damage was clean, attractive wood just waiting to be revealed. About five hours later and after some reassembly, it looked like a whole new table. My back ached, my hands were numb, my joints rattled, and I had a lot of sawdust up my nose (Are you familiar with the term woodshop buggers?), but it was so worth it. This thing looked gorgeous.

I stained it. Ah. There was that attractive wood grain and natural beauty we had once known. After a double coat of lacquer, the surface looked like glass. I glowed with satisfaction. My wife would be home shortly. I knew she would be pleased. Except for the dusty garage, but you have to break a few eggs if you want to make an omelet.

I set the table into its place in the dining room and stepped back to enjoy what I had accomplished. "That's two brownie points for Ben," I muttered to myself. "I mean, the table even matches the new chairs now." That's high-class living, am I right?

All the remnants of twenty years of service to the Higgins family had been removed. Our table looked great. I felt a twinge of loss and that caught me by surprise. The table had had so much personality, and such a rich story to tell. Now it just looked amazing. Before, it sang the epic poetry of time and life well lived. Now it just glowed attractively. What had I done? What had been lost? How strange the things we miss when they are gone. The dents were tangible connections to the past, our precious family story in wooden scars. The burns had served as markers for memory and cues to retell the events. Each nick...

I glanced outside to make sure my wife hadn't come home yet, went to the silverware drawer, found a fork, and took it to our new table. Slowly, I turned it upside down in my hand and paused over the pristine, glossy surface. And...I definitely did not stab my table! Are you crazy? Do you know how much work it takes to refinish a kitchen table? I'm not insane, but I considered it. So maybe I am.

MUSTARD AND PICKLE SANDWICHES

Have you ever had someone engage you in conversation and from word one you could tell they just wanted to fight? Sometimes this happens to me. The person searches for a point of conflict or offense so they can pounce and go at me. It feels like being hunted. I imagine it's a little like how the gazelle must feel with the lion. Chase, bite, and eat. Hey, I don't want to fight!

Let's examine the lion's personality and how we should respond when we are the gazelle. Let's start with the wide-angle culture lens and then zoom in slowly to the family and the heart.

I often dive into controversy by mistake by making generalized claims that others find offensive. People get riled up over the smallest things. For example, if I claim that "a day well-lived includes learning something new," they might get miffed. "Are you trying to say I'm wasting my life? Who are you to judge me? That's so offensive. You shouldn't make generalizations."

If I laugh because I think they must be joking, they get angrier. They're serious, I realize too late. How can they be offended by a proverb that proclaims learning enhances the quality of life? It makes no sense to get angry at that. In preaching the value of learning, am I insulting anyone? Not in normal times and not with normal people. "Are you calling me NOT normal? What am I stupid? You think I'm dumb?" The Hyper Sensitive Mafia has become so loud in our culture today. They delight in twisting benign speech into offense? It's the relational equivalent of a mustard and pickle sandwich. It's designed to stir up trouble and leave stains.

These trolls have taught me my "something new" for today. Some folks believe "a day well lived includes being offended, arguing, or asserting power over others by bullying them into silence." It's unfortunate but true. Jerks are everywhere. They like muddying the well. They enjoy sowing dissent, conflict, and division. At the risk of using too many metaphors, some people like breaking other people's toys. These people are constantly pushing friends away and having to find new ones. Use, abuse, replace is the pattern for this personality. It's not a fulfilling way to live. The best thing we can do is refuse to take their mustard and pickle sandwiches and avoid them. Right?

Social media is an excellent place to observe these people in bulk on an hourly basis. One person wants to encourage, educate, connect, or improve the world. They post something like, "How would the world change if everyone became lifelong learners?" A second person who views the internet as a place to gain notoriety by throwing virtual sand in the eyes of the innocent trolls for victims. It's their blood sport. They insult, argue, undermine, censor, and bully with a grin on their face. The best thing we can do is ignore and block these people. Right?

Sure, the process has a lot of entertainment value for the general population like MMA, boxing, and shark attacks. Unengaged third parties sense the conflict brewing, form a circle, and chant, "Fight, fight, fight." I find social media so saturated with the bad behavior of morally bankrupt people that I avoid the digital town squares completely. I recommend that others do the same.

So, with a casual conversation, we can break off, and with online slime, we can log off, but what about with family? What if this dynamic exists in our closest relationships? That's when this problem becomes serious. What if you can't avoid them? If it doesn't rise to the level of abuse, not that that is a very clear line, but it does feel predatory. How do you cope? It's like they view you as the emotional gazelle to their lion. The mustard and pickle sandwiches are piling up and you don't know what to do with all of them.

This is the process I'm learning. I'm just a Padawan, so nothing is mastered yet. Still, I think it is a good guide.

Step one. Check yourself before you wreck yourself. Okay, it happened. I feel like Mr. Crapinski. My emotions scream out for a guilty verdict and execution. Red lights are flashing. Time to stop and check myself. I find this step excruciating after I've been wronged. I'm feeling John Wick, not Jesus Christ. I get off by myself, breathe, and consider Matthew 7:3-5 which says, "Why do you look at the speck of sawdust in your brother's eye and pay no attention to the plank in your own eye?" What does that tell me? Check myself. Change me first. It is easy to misread situations like this in a way that absolves me from guilt. I know I didn't start it, but I could still have a plank in my eye. Its removal is my first priority.

Step two. "if it is possible, as far as it depends on you, live at peace with everyone." That comes from the Bible too, Romans 12:18. "As far as it depends on you," means I might need to apologize for how I handled myself while under the attack from an aggressor. I rarely do it perfectly. Did I enflame the issue? I probably did. I consider this and try to do it better next time. I try to be more patient. I try to hold my tongue. I try to understand the other side. I try to prevent biting words from escaping my lips. Try is the operative word. I know the lion is going to come after me again in a month, a week, or tomorrow, but I am striving to be fleet on my feet, graceful under pressure, and also avoid having my guts ripped out. When I handle my side of the argument better, sometimes the fight doesn't happen. That's the goal. "A gentle answer turns away wrath, but a harsh word stirs up anger," Proverb 15:1.

Step three: Forgive. I might need to ask for forgiveness from the lion even though I did not start the fight. We are talking about people after all, and the family aggressor often gets hurt too. That is hard for me. I much prefer it when I handle things more cleanly. Then all I need to deal with is another mustard and pickle sandwich. You can't do anything with those sandwiches, they're garbage, but the bill for them is due. Someone has got to pay the bill. Sure, the lion should pay for them, but he's not going to. He might not even know how many sandwiches he left behind.

You only have two choices. Do nothing. Ignore them. Let them rot. They'll stink up your soul. They turn to bitterness so quickly it's insane. There is nothing that destroys your quality of life like unresolved mustard and pickle sandwiches. Trust me, you don't want that kind of garbage piling up in your life. So what's the other option? Pay the bill and dispose of the sandwiches. "Wait, why should I have to pay when the lion hurt me!"

You don't have to pay the bill but it's the only way to get rid of the mustard and pickle sandwiches and not ruin the rest of your life. Seriously, for once, I'm not being hyperbolic. Forgiveness is the only way to avoid the rot of bitterness that eats your soul over time.

A story to consider while you are struggling through this step. Yes, you will struggle every time with this step. I do. We all do. That's just reality. Read the Parable of the Unmerciful Servant in Matthew 18: 21-35. We have been forgiven an uncountable mountain of debt, so we must forgive the pocket change of hurts that people owe us.

It really is a good day when we learn something new. What would the world look like if lions learned to leave the gazelles alone, the gazelles learned to forgive the lions, and everyone stopped ordering those diabolical mustard and pickle sandwiches?

DO YOU PANIC OR PARTY?

I remember the first time the power blinked out with each of my young kids. They weren't sure what had happened. In their limited experience, everything doesn't just go dark. Power outages usually occured during winter windstorms. In Anchorage, that meant the wind was howling over the edges of our house, all the roof vents were rattling, and the darkness of night went on and on. I could see how this would seem scary to a toddler, but the fix for their fears was simple, raid the cupboard with the flashlights, lanterns, and candles and throw a Power Out Party.

Soon the living room bathed in the soft, flickering glow of a single flame and the kids were exploring the house by the narrow beam of a flashlight. As I watched, I remembered being a kid doing the same thing. Do you remember how the house transformed in total darkness? The familiar became spooky, but you had a light to navigate by. You felt nervous and brave at the same time. You discovered cobwebs dangling from the corners of the ceiling that you had somehow never seen by the light of the electric bulbs. Your room was a cave. The bathroom was a cavern. The garage was a den. The backyard was a jungle.

When the power goes out, do you panic or party?

I grab a flashlight, find the couch, and watch the Hyper Kids show. And that cobweb. In the beam of my light, I can't unsee it. How am I going to get that thing off the vaulted ceiling? A broom, I decide. Should I do it now? Nah, we are in the middle of a Power Out Party. Get it later. Once the power goes back on, you won't notice it anyway. May as well just leave it. There is a lot of dust gathering on those light fixtures too. My family is sloughing too many skin cells again.

It's funny how darkness forces a different perspective on the familiar rooms of the house. This thought gets my mind rabbit trailing. Then I'm thinking about how I'm thinking, why I'm thinking, and what that says about me. Metacognition is the longest rabbit trail of all.

Power Out Parties are the best!

Michelle, my wife, usually gets worried during power outages. What if the power doesn't come back on? The heat doesn't work without the electricity. Will we end up wearing parkas and snow gear in the house? What about the food in the refrigerator? Will it spoil? She is usually in the middle of a task that the outage interrupts. This is inconvenient. She rushes around the house trying to adapt to the new state of the play. She is flustered. The kids generally want all kinds of stuff. Can we get this out? Can we do that? I want a flashlight too. The batteries are dead. My flashlight stopped working.

My wife runs around trying to meet every need. I'm a dad so my response is more like, "That's unfortunate! What are you going to do about it?" "You don't NEED your own flashlight, you WANT one." "We've got days before anything starts spoiling, but we should probably start in on the ice cream now."

I'm sure my wife appreciates my perspective in times like this. I think I really contribute to the family dynamic during Power Out Parties. My phone has plenty of battery left. "How about some music!"

Pretty soon we are dancing through the house by candlelight, making memories, strobing the flashlight so the living room looks like a discotheque, and eating cookies and cream. This is the Father of the Year award type of leadership, I know.

My honey gets the last things situated about the same time as the lights flick back on. The microwave beeps. The refrigerator compressor kicks on. She looks frustrated. Now she has to put everything away again. "Power is back!" I announce.

My kids cry out, "Uh. No fair! We were playing,"

"Power Out Parties are unpredictable," I reply.

The kids inevitably whine. "Dad, can we turn out all the lights?"

I look at my wife. She sighs and nods. We turn out all the lights. That's when the magic happens. My wife transforms from a worker bee into a party animal. Before long we are all laughing and singing. The lights may be on across the street but the Power Out Party keeps raging in the Higgins house.

BABY PROBLEMS AND SUPER MOMMAS

Did you know the world has a baby problem? I can't browse YouTube without noticing at least one video about demographic collapse. Apparently, to keep a population stable a country needs 2.1 births per woman and many parts of the world are not keeping up with that level of reproduction to support their current levels of infrastructure and government spending. It would seem that we are in danger of some major problems. Interesting. Doom, gloom, and catastrophe loom.

I don't pretend to be an expert in demography, but my wife and I have managed to double the replacement standard and are working hard to make our kids excellent additions to the citizen pool through our top-tier homeschooling, by teaching the Bible, and making parenting decisions with our generational legacy in mind. I am happy to report that all four of our children are real "keepers." I think this gives me the right to have a strong opinion on the baby problem.

I'm not sure if the world's baby problem stems from our prosperity (the richer people grow the fewer children they tend to have), our urbanization (city dwellers tend toward fewer children than normal folks-I meant to say rural dwellers), our growing amorality (which tends to encourage the pushing off of marriage and children until later in life to pursue work, pleasure, or experience in the prime of life), environmental contaminants (microplastics in our bodies doesn't sound like a good thing for fertility), or our over comfort with killing 73 million of our babies per year (according to the World Health Organization). Strong opinions abound on all these subjects on the YouTubes. Perhaps all these things play a role in our baby problem.

If we didn't destroy 73 million success stories before they got a foothold outside the womb, perhaps world demographic decline wouldn't be a thing. Bad government policies have certainly also played a role in the baby problem. From the one-child policy in China which forced the demographic crisis, they find themselves in today to governments' immoral management of fiat currency at the expense of their citizen's financial health. Ever heard someone quote a financial statistic from thirty years ago and then immediately quote the equivalent in today's inflated dollars? The dollar has lost around 90% of its buying power during my lifetime according to CPI data.

In my parents' generation, a one-income family was more possible, but our declining buying power necessitates two-worker households in many cases and has pressed children out of the equation more and more. All this is to say that if we wanted to fix the baby problem through public policy, we could. I doubt we will if past precedent holds. Let's say, I'm not holding my breath.

I think there is a far more corrosive cause of the baby problem, and it is one we can do something about. We've stopped honoring motherhood as the most valuable institution in the world. We've denigrated the work they do and convinced girls that doing anything else would be a "something better" life choice. What pure lunacy. If it is true that we get more of the things we honor, then perhaps each of us can do something to fix this baby problem. Give motherhood the undisputed crown of honor it deserves.

I recently watched a TV show, which got my mind spinning on this topic, where the mother character's reason for being in the script was to complain about motherhood. The show creators clearly viewed the series as their pulpit to preach feminism. Oh, how the exhausted mom wished she could get out of the house and smoke crack, drink, sleep around, and act like an idiot college sorority sister. Motherhood was all stress and fatigue and no joy, purpose, or deep human connection. The mom ended up puking into a toilet in front of her confused kid and dumbfounded husband. A real wake-up call? I doubt it, given the writers of that show.

Let's be honest about motherhood. It is exhausting. It is stressful. Parenting has probably been one of the hardest things my wife and I have done in our lives, but it is also the most important thing. It is an honorable thing, a useful thing, and a beautiful thing. Without mothers, the world ends. Just remember that when you're doom-scrolling through today's news. I think it is time we flip the script on our culture and begin honoring the mothers amongst us as the real heroes who don't wear capes.

Toward that end, I would like to nominate someone for "The Mom Of The Day" award. She demonstrated motherly grit, ingenuity, and grace under pressure at Costco yesterday.

I was sitting in front of the hotdog counter watching the never-ending train of people and carts waiting to have their receipts checked at the exit. I saw a woman carrying a baby in a front pack towing her cart full of groceries behind her. My eyes trailed backward in the line and I noticed something impressive. Using a strap, the mother had rigged a way to tow a stroller behind her cart like a railroad car. It followed exactly behind the cart. I thought this was a very cool idea. I glanced back at the mother. Her face was calm and collected. This seemed admirable to me as the Costco crowd usually has me feeling frazzled even without my kids in tow.

The train moved forward a few paces. I looked back to the stroller. The content four or five-year-old sat in the stroller, looking like a happy tourist at the zoo. He looked around and watched all the people munching on hot dogs and pizza. This mom had solved the age-old problem of how to get groceries in if your kids want to ride in the cart. Very admirable, but she wasn't done impressing.

She pulled the train up a few more feet and handed her receipt to the Costco employee. I noticed she had another kid in tow, a second stroller was tied behind the first stroller. This truly was a train and I had found the caboose. The occupant of the last car in the train was a one or two-year-old kid.

"What a cool setup?" I thought to myself. An older sibling stood beside the toddler's car, leaning over to talk and play with the young one. Maybe I caught them at a good moment, but the four kids all looked content and mom didn't look stressed at all. What an accomplishment.

I pointed out the mother and her kid train to my eighteen-year-old daughter who had just returned from "ketchup" ing her dog. "How impressive is that?"

This mother deserves a lot of respect for the work she is doing for us. Yes, her work directly benefits us because she is our neighbor, generally speaking. Her kids are our future. If she teaches them well, our future has great promise. If she screws up her children's lives, our future is diminished. I'm not saying anything you don't already know. Mothers make the future and write its story. We depend on them. It's about time we heaped honor, recognition, and help on the heads of the mothers in our circles of influence. You can start making a difference in the world today by nominating someone for "The Mother Of The Day" award and letting others know about it.

If our culture started treating motherhood as the center of the universe, perhaps all the policy issues in our world would fall into line. After all, the things that you give honor to will abound evermore.

BATS BY THE BILLIONS

My family had spent the day at Six Flags Discovery Kingdom in California. The sky glowed pink with dusky light as I drove the hour back to our hotel in Rancho Cordova. The rental car and the roads were unfamiliar so I felt thankful for the remaining light. I hoped it would hold until we arrived.

My wife and kids were exhausted from the day and hungry. They inhaled the Costco hot dogs and cheese pizza I had picked up before collecting them outside the gate. As we passed between vast flooded rice fields, I saw a wisp of smoke crossing the highway in the distance.

I looked closer and it seemed strange. It didn't have the texture and pattern of smoke. It looked too thin and it was moving wrong. No, it couldn't be smoke. As my speed ate up the distance, it began to look more like an undulating black ribbon streaming over the road a mile ahead. Then I saw a fluttering in the smoke and my eyes refocused from the whole to the parts. Wings. Tens of thousands of fluttering wings.

"Look, kids!" I pointed out through the windshield.

"What is that?" We wondered.

"Birds, I think it is tens of thousands of birds," I suggested as I noticed the ribbon of flyers originated in a grove of trees and were fanning out over the rice paddies. I studied the shape of their wings and the cadence of their flapping while staying within my lane. The wings were wrong for birds. "Bats!" I exclaimed. "It's tens of thousands of bats all going out for the night at once."

We passed directly under the swarm. It was a majestic moment. The sunset. The bats. I felt like I was in a nature documentary. "Wow! That is amazing."

Then Sam, my sixteen-year-old son said, "It's not tens of thousands. Thousands maybe, but not tens of thousands."

I was jolted from the grandeur of the moment. "I think there are more than it seems. Each bat is so small. That is a lot of bats. Tens of thousands."

"No Dad. Just thousands." The thick traffic hurled onward, a ribbon of hundreds of vehicles heading into the darkness, not to hunt mosquitos in the rice fields but to find homes and beds. The nocturnal bats and diurnal humans, pass like ships in the night.

Maybe, he was right. I remembered that it was usually a bad bet to counter Sam's call regarding anything mathematical. My family accuses me of exaggerating in my storytelling all the time. Wait, that's probably another exaggeration. All the time is literally without stopping. My family doesn't accuse me of exaggerating ALL the time. Gosh, this is frustrating. I mean it more figuratively. Often. Sometimes. Occasionally. That one time. For crying out loud, I'm not doing math here! It's just storytelling.

As I navigated to Rancho Cordova, I thought about my creative mind and how it worked so differently from Sam's, or my wife's for that matter. To say tens of thousands of bats, for me, is to communicate the feeling of the great swarm of them. I wanted to communicate the feeling of grandeur that electrified the very ribs in my chest. Not, literally. It's a metaphor. Illustration. Comparison. The spectacular moment that I experienced can not be communicated emotionally and with precision. I may as well have said "Bats by the billions." After all, with three repeating B's in a line, you get some extra pizzazz.

But some people think in concrete numbers, precise quantities, absolute absolutes, and unwavering accuracy. "Was that in grams or ounces?"

"Was that three thousand meters or yards?"

I am glad we have logical minds like Sam's, the world is built on the precision of their thoughts, but I think there is also a place for an occasional hyperbolic story. Without the dreamer, the storyteller, and the exaggerators what would this world be like? Boring for one. Without inspiration, for another.

But..just to prove that we dreamers and storytellers aren't

completely unmoored from reality, I did a little research and found that we were driving near the Yolo Bypass Wildlife Area. According to the California Department of Fish and Wildlife website, "250,000 Mexican free-tailed bats choose the Yolo Causeway as their home." Wait a minute! Did the dreamer just find a piece of data that makes his numbers probable? Let's read on. "There are foraging opportunities nearby and the adjacent wetlands and rice fields are a food source for insects." Did the hyperbole guy accurately explain why the bats were heading toward the rice fields? What?!

Now, I'm no mathematician Sam, but I'd say that 250,000 bats could be accurately expressed as "tens of thousands." Just saying! That's one small point for this storyteller but one giant leap for exaggerating kind!

THE SILLY, THE GOOFY, AND THE GROSS

"But it's disgusting!" My mother/editor said.

"It IS disgusting. That's what makes it funny," I retorted.

In the video chat, it seemed obvious that she disagreed. I think my sense of humor is a little twisted.

I'd just finished helping my daughter write a book called, The Adventures of Poop Turd, where an enthusiastic turd comes to life and joins a little boy's family. They have many gross adventures together that read a little like Calvin and Hobbs, except a lot messier.

My eight-year-old daughter and I enjoyed thinking up and writing the book together. She dictated the story. I typed, cleaned up the grammar, and guided the narrative flow. It was only after it was "published" that we realized other people don't appreciate the same type of humor that we do.

I suppose I could have guessed from my mother's reaction. Oops. A minor oversight on my part. I still think it will make an excellent animated TV show.

The problem is me, I admit it. I've got the sense of humor of a ten-year-old boy. A psychoanalyst might link it back to my childhood or my father who told his share of gross-out jokes too. When I was younger, my mom called it bathroom humor, perhaps to sanitize them as much as possible. Apparently, fart jokes aren't everyone's cup of tea. I can't figure out why. My mom tolerated my dad's jokes when I was a kid just like my wife tolerates mine. The generational cycle of humor continues. If I am successful, my great-grandchildren will giggle over hilarious potty jokes too. Through my sense of humor, I believe I am making a positive contribution to the world. It is my purpose, my WHY.

Several people have said that identifying humor is like seeing great art, when you see it, you just know it. This rings true with most of mine but doesn't help me pin down what makes things funny. Beauty is in the eye of the beholder. Humor is in the mind of the listener. However, I would add it's also in my mind as the joke teller. When I tell a nice gross-out joke, I enjoy myself thoroughly.

But let's get serious about this for a minute. According to the Humor Research Lab at the University of Colorado Boulder, "humor occurs when and only when three conditions are satisfied: 1) a situation is a violation, 2) the situation is benign, and 3) both perceptions occur simultaneously." I find the idea that a University would give humor serious study to be hilarious, but they have so there you go.

According to the Benign Violation Theory, to be funny something needs to be a violation of social, cultural, linguistic, logical, or moral norms and present no real danger at the same time.

What do you find funny? It would seem that all our different tastes in humor depend on which norm we enjoy the benign violation of. If you like to violate linguistic norms, you're a 'pun'ster. If you like to violate moral norms, you'll probably laugh at bedroom humor. There are plenty of cultural norms to be poked at. Don't forget about them. Although, during my lifetime, I have noticed a lot of people have lost their sense of humor.

It would seem that not everyone agrees on the definition of benign, and that is a real shame. By the way, it means, "Gentle. Kindly. Not harmful in effect." I think some folks use humor as a weapon to bully, trade barbs, and inflict personal insults. Laughing at people is not funny because it's not benign. It's a violation that causes harm. Not funny. The best way to stop this brand of non-humor is to refuse to laugh.

On the other hand, these days the political mafia uses manufactured outrage, fake offense, and the imagined insults of benign humor as a method of gaining power. "You hurt my feelings, you must be silenced." I find this trend to be more disgusting than a badly timed diarrhea joke.

In a world that increasingly seems to have its panties in a wad, I retreat to simpler times and more ridiculous humor. Do you remember the good old days when we could cluster together on the playground and just laugh at fart jokes? I do. Good times.

Our book, The Adventures of Poop Turd violates social norms for polite conversation. Flatulence and bathroom topics are utter violations in grocery stores, libraries, airplanes, and public swimming pools. So we squirm at the violation while knowing it is not real and therefore not dangerous. We are grossed out, but not offended.

I've never lost my love for the silly, the goofy, and the gross. The way I see it, if the world is so full of the ridiculous, why not enjoy it? If you let yourself stay young at heart, you'll find there is always something to laugh about. Humor abounds.

WE'RE A FLIPPIN' BOTTLE FLIPPING FAMILY

Memorable moments in my family usually sneak up on me.

We were at the Higgins family reunion in Redding, California. The heat had kept me inside for most of the day, but at around seven thirty, I noticed Olivia, my eighteen-year-old daughter, outside in the decorative, white-gravel garden. She sat, surrounded by Liquid Amber trees, in the centermost spot of three low benches. Most of the family had gone home, so the socializing frenzy that characterizes our reunions had given way to quiet reflection.

I meandered outside. The assaulting heat of the day had begun to relent. I slipped my feet into flip-flops and walked out to her. The light was gentle on the rustling leaves around the rock garden. In the distance, I could hear birds over the beaver pond on Churn Creek.

Olivia held a cup of ice cream, which she had layered sliced nectarines into with her usual artistic flare. I watched her nibbling contentedly. Sitting on a bench close by, I watched her savoring the dessert. We chatted quietly and sat together. I was struck with a sense of quiet contentment and joy, which is usual when I'm around her. She's just that kind of person.

A few minutes later, my wife found us in the garden and sat close to me. "I'm going on my walk," she informed us, but she didn't rush off. It felt as if the magnetism of the place held her and she snuggled close to me, laying a head on my shoulder. My wife is usually a mover and a shaker, but something about the garden, or the moment helped her settle against my side and I remembered the "all is right" ness I'd felt the first time she lay her head on my shoulder twenty-eight year before in a different garden, in a different city, at the start of another evening when the oppressive heat of the day had just begun to wane. That was when I first knew she was the one for me.

My wife, Olivia, and I chatted softly in the garden. The reunion food had been too good. "It's like going on a cruise," I suggested. "Great food, all the time."

"That's why I need to take a walk," my wife said but she didn't move away from me, which I liked.

Sam, my sixteen-year-old son, came out from the house carrying two water bottles. He gave one to Olivia and immediately started bantering with her. The energy of the garden livened, as is usual when my son is around. I was struck with a deep-seated thankfulness that my two "Olders" had such a good rapport. The stereotypical teen angst, sibling rivalry, and relational nightmares had not materialized in my family. What a tremendous gift, I thought while I watched them giggle and tease. Sam initiated, as usual. Olivia tolerated and reciprocated, as is her way.

Olivia guzzled most of her water bottle. She'd gotten dehydrated from the California heat. "If I had my Chosen mug, this wouldn't have happened," she explained. She tended to sip more from her super cool "Stanley-style," Chosen Merch, triple insulated, supersized mug.

Sam grabbed Olivia's quarter-filled bottle, screwed the cap down hard, and began flipping it through the air so that it would land upright. Thump. Thump. I was reminded of weeks and months in the past when our house was filled with the bang and thump of water bottle flipping practice. Sam landed one on the third or fourth try. He missed the next one and the bottle rolled against Olivia's foot. She tried a flip. Smack. The bottle nearly landed but over-rotated and rolled to Mom's foot. Michelle picked it up and tried to flip the bottle. Boom. She landed it, which made her puff her feathers like the cock of the walk. I felt obligated to show everyone how bottle flipping was done. "I'll show you how to do it," I announced and flung it as high as I could, over our heads and into the boxwood hedge.

"Dad!" Olivia shrieked.

I laughed. Sam retrieved the bottle and the bottle flipping continued around the circle. Sam landed another. Olivia came so close. Michelle learned that she had been "first-time lucky." I flung it as high as I could again and it smashed the cap in. Sam reshaped the neck of the bottle and restarted the cycle. We laughed and flipped and cheered and laughed some more, all caught up in this ridiculously perfect family moment. After about a hundred flips and several more cap crashes, the water started leaking from the lid, but that didn't phase us.

My chest filled with proud papa joy and I declared, "We are a flippin' bottle-flipping family."

Olivia and Sam froze and stared at me and then over at Mom. Michelle enforces a very conservative line on cussing. The word "crap" is over the line, but nonsensical expletives like "Crumb Sclubbit" might be okay.

"Did I go too far?"

Sam marked a spot in the air with one hand and pointed just below the mark with his other hand. "It's right on the edge, Dad."

I laughed, thoroughly enjoying this family dynamic in the dusky garden and, of course, my Dad Joke. "But we are a flippin' bottle-flipping family."

The bottle game continued. I reflected as I observed their joking, not everyone has such a flippin' awesome family. Sometimes, it's good for me to take a breath and appreciate moments like these. To slow all the moving and shaking just long enough to savor the flavor of an artistically pleasing, perfectly presented, wonderfully sweet family moment. A Johnson Oatman Jr. song comes to mind, "Count your blessings. Name them one by one. Count your blessings. See what God hath done."

I feel so thankful for my family and all the years we might have to master the sport of bottle flipping. Perhaps someday we will join the circus as The Flippin' Bottle Flipping Higgins Family Dynamos. You never know. It could happen.

WHERE MY HEART FINDS ITS HOME

Spring had finally arrived after a long winter with near-record-breaking snowfall. The excitement of seeing sidewalk concrete instead of snow berms and asphalt instead of road ice nudged me toward the great Alaskan outdoors. If I were a real Alaskan, I would not let the weather dictate my outdoor recreation, but I tend to hibernate in my cave during the dark, cold winters. I know. I am embarrassed enough, don't rub it in.

I can't begin to explain the elation of the first sunlight that brings warmth to the cheek in spring. It's like tasting chocolate for the first time, or some other divine gift. You might understand why I would immediately want to get out in the woods and bask in the promise of summer.

I untied my e-bike from the ceiling of my garage where it had hung since October like a butchered chicken in a Mexican street market. The roads had not been swept of traction gravel and the temperature had barely risen over forty degrees, but it was time to take my first ride of the season.

Before you get the wrong idea about me, let me explain. I'm a thinker, not an athlete. I'm decidedly non-competitive and I can't fathom the high my brother-in-law gets from conquering summits. I don't ride my bike in the woods to beat yesterday's time. If I were a mattress, I'd be more soft than firm. I didn't even discover the miles of trails right by my house for the first twenty years that we lived here.

Costco's decision to sell e-bikes and a stash of "fun money" burning a hole in my pocket changed all that. I had my way into the woods. More importantly, I had my way back out of the woods. In Alaska, the wilderness can kill you a mile from home just as well as in the middle of nowhere. With the assistance of my tiny peddle-assist bike, I began exploring the wood's trails. What a game-changer!

I experienced again the feelings of boyhood, being in the woods had always been like a cradle for my soul. Soothing. Calming. Home. Now, I could whisk myself along gravel paths, along rivers, and past spectacular, million-dollar vistas without all the work of hauling my carcass up the hills. Utterly transformative.

I began on the shortest trails, unsure how long my battery would last. You don't want this battery to run empty, it will destroy your legs trying to peddle a dead e-bike home. Ask me how I learned that little morsel of wisdom. That's right, the hard way. But usually, my e-bike rides are glorious. I can ride right next to a swamp in the middle of summer and not get a single mosquito bite. "Catch me if you can, blood-suckers! Ha. Ha!"

I get mixed reactions from the others on the trail. From "that's an interesting tiny bike that that large man is riding" to "there's no way he's going to get up that hill on that bike, oh... he did" to a sort of disapproval and irritation from the real cyclists who view the sport through the purity lens. "E-bikes are a menace and a corruption of the cycling lifestyle." They are probably right, but those tight, spandex outfits they've been subjecting all of us to have always felt like a violation of proper "men's attire" to me, so I figure we're even.

As the trees fly past, all the stress of the city melts away. The concentration of staying on the winding path requires total focus. The wildlife provides nice surprises. I haven't had a mama brown bear surprise yet, here's hoping I don't. I'm pretty sure some hiker got mauled a couple of years ago, but let's not think about that. I have run across several mama moose on the trail. Thankfully, all the trails are loops and I can just go around the other way.

Mostly, I just love the character of a real forest. Not a city park, the natural woods. Fallen trees with roots splayed into the air, mushrooms consuming the rotting wood. Disorder and life growing everywhere in the midst of it. The birds. The sun cutting through the canopy. And certainly, the gentle respite from the sounds of car tires on roadways. My heart finds peace in the woods.

I am pretty sure I started this article with a plan to bring some serious life issues into my forest e-biking metaphor, but that seems wrong now. Does everything need to be serious? Why can't I just savor the feeling of the spring sun, God's great creation, my tiny e-bike, and the miracle of engineering that allows that little motor to carry me up and down some extremely sketchy gravel trails?

MY ESOPHAGUS PASSWORD

My esophagus has a password that I keep forgetting. Yesterday, while eating a plate of pulled pork soft tacos, I downed an enthusiastic bite and reached for my water glass. I felt pressure behind my ribs. When I tried to wash the Mexican food down I got the equivalent of that little refusal shake that the password box on my computer does when I type in the wrong password. The water splashed against the blockage deep in my throat unable to get into my stomach. With no place to go it just sat there, sloshing around. That disconcerting feeling when a normal body process unexpectedly fails is like a computer throwing up an error message. "Incorrect esophageal password, please proceed to the nearest bathroom for ten minutes of discomfort and reverse thrusters."

People hear about my swallowing disorder and usually think I could choke. My dad imagined that I had passed out on the floor of the restaurant bathroom and came to check on me. No, my pulled pork tacos aren't stuck in my airway, for which I am thankful and because of which I am still alive. I tried to explain this to him, "I'm okay, just...have...to let...my body...puke it up...takes time."

I stood over the toilet and waited for my body to initiate the reverse thruster protocol. It's an uncomfortable waiting process and it's not pretty, so I assume you'll appreciate my not describing it here. You're welcome.

There is a treatment for the scar tissue that is building inside my esophagus. A doctor can slide a balloon down my throat and blow it up until it rips the inflexible scar tissue apart, thereby allowing my muscles to swallow as they should. Of course, it's only a temporary fix. Soon new scar tissue will develop and my swallowing trouble will return. Do you understand my hesitancy to have the procedure done?

Actually, I self-administered this procedure once by accident. Not with a balloon. Gosh, that makes me gag just thinking about it. No, I took a giant gulp of water once and felt a white-hot knife of pain from my neck to my stomach as the scar tissue tore all the way down. It felt like I had strep throat for a few days afterward, but once it healed I could swallow normally for about six months. I saved some money with that ordeal, but it was horrible.

So, I must remember my swallowing password and manage my condition. Small bites, well chewed. A drink of water between swallows. Avoid all foods that cause allergic reactions. When I haven't eaten for a while, start with nibbles to remind my esophagus how to work correctly. This is difficult for me as I am a wolf when it comes to food. Taking delicate nibbles goes against my default programming. But, every error message from my esophagus is another reminder that I am not a wolf but a man with Eosinophilic Esophagitis.

As I returned to my plate of pulled pork soft tacos, I considered how I should proceed and why I had to have so many chronic health issues. I minced up the dish so it resembled the food you'd feed to a teething toddler. Careful now. Don't get too crazy and load a whole fork full. As to my other question? That's a tougher one.

"Why?" is a difficult question to answer with any degree of satisfaction. Why do bad things happen? People have rejected God over this question. Other people have found God as a response to this question. I've wrestled with it for thirty-six years. It's a loaded question, an issue of the heart.

But actually, I'm not really wondering why bad things happen. I'm asking why they happen to me, aren't I? The truth is that I don't want to suffer. I don't want to wait. I don't want to fail. I don't want to get sick. I want good things. I want ease. I want health and prosperity. "Why me?" my heart groans.

If I did not suffer, would I be so concerned with the question of why bad things happen? Wouldn't that be someone else's problem? Like when a genocide takes place on the other side of the world and you hear of it in passing, you don't enter into the tragedy. "How terrible," you may say but that is all you feel.

Would I care as much for the suffering of others if I did not suffer too? The person in the booth behind me is probably suffering through an abusive marriage. The old guy with the walker has an arthritic back. The server could be struggling to provide for his family while feeling trapped in a job he hates. The cook is smiling through the pain of a burnt finger. The homeless guy outside is trapped in a drug addiction that has torpedoed his dreams and destroyed his family.

Today, I think that maybe it is good that I have a swallowing disorder among my many other ailments. If for no other reason than so I can properly learn compassion for others.

Going further still, perhaps my difficulty and suffering are a kind of gift. Without it's education, I could not truly enter into the lives of others. We are bonded together during the battle with our infirmities. We are built in our crucibles of pain. To walk with a friend in their suffering is the greatest good we can do in life. In other words, my pain helps me love others better. Suffering still stinks and I hate it, but...well, you get it. Two opposing things can exist at the same time in the human heart.

In case you were wondering, the pulled pork soft tacos were delicious! Five stars! Highly recommend.

MY FUNNEL THEORY OF CLUTTER

My house is the Hotel California for stuff. "You can check out but you can never leave." Winter gear for example is a particularly gnarly problem. The coats are hung five deep on every wall peg. The boot rack looks like it has been eaten by a blob monster consisting of boots, beanies, mismatched gloves, dust, road gravel, and, of course, more coats. I think there is a R/C car under there. Throw in a bow and arrow, an airsoft rifle, and a telephone and you get the picture. Over the seven months of winter, our garage becomes an abomination of desolation. I can't walk without tripping over something.

A week ago, I tried to navigate through the garage and my gorge rose. Now, I am not a clean freak, but this has gotten out of control. I pulled a kindergarten-sized school chair out from under a pile of wet gloves and sat in front of the mess. Thankfully, the small chair held my considerable weight. I assumed the thinking position. Something must be done, or this stuff will eat us next. Solutions began dancing through my head, which happens when I assume the thinking position. I could build a floor-to-ceiling shelving system to take advantage of the only space left in my house, the vertical space, but the real problem was the clutter.

Did we need ten coats for each person? I have worn maybe two of mine, but new ones came into the house faster than the old jackets wore out. This is even though I don't recall ever buying myself a winter jacket. They just appear, I think. It's the magical hand-me-down fairy.

For example, last year my dad gave me a brand new Carhartt jacket that I love. It will probably take fifteen years to wear it out, so we should probably toss all the older ones. I'm set in the coat department until my youngest graduates high school, according to my math. I am in the thinking position after all. The brilliance of a lightbulb flashes above my head. "Maybe if we just got rid of the old stuff our house wouldn't be so maddeningly cluttered. What genius is this?"

I stand up and congratulate myself for identifying the solution. Then I remember who I married and sit back down in the thinking chair. My wife doesn't like the term "hoarder," so I try not to use it, but she is definitely reluctant to let anything leave the house that might be needed at any point in the future. Is that a diplomatic way of stating it? It's almost like she is the narrow part of a funnel, standing guard by the exit sign, which reads, "Nothing leaves except by the express permission of the High Regent, Lord Emperor."

On the reverse side of this sign, another message reads, "Give me your old stuff, your hand-me-downs, Your huddled masses of things yearning for a new home. The wretched refuse of your basements. Send these, the homeless, tempest-tossed items to me, I lift my lamp beside the golden door!"

My wife created the funnel. It's too easy for stuff to get in and too hard for anything to get out. With the things we buy added into the mix, the entrance side of the funnel is wide open. Too wide. And the exit side of the funnel is narrow. Too narrow. As I sit in my thinking position, I concoct a new plan. The only way to fix this situation is to influence The High Lord Regent into letting some things go.

I must infect her mind with an idea virus, like in that Inception movie. The Spring Cleaning Decluttering Bug. That's SCDB-24 for short, not that that helps. Once she contracts the decluttering bug, she'll scour the whole house and the exit side of the funnel will widen for a short window of time. During this week, if I'm a lucky boy, we might be able to throw some old stuff away. Oh. What a sweet idea! I imagine clutter-free walkways and shelves with a little open space. My heart twitterpated a bit. As cruel as it may seem to purposely infect the person I love with a virus, it must be done.

She walks into the garage to pull a loaf of bread from the freezer. "You know, Honey?" I mention off-handedly. "if I built a bigger, better boot shelf, I think the garage could be much more organized." I scratch my scruffy beard and try to look non-nonchalant. Her hoarder immune system could reject the virus or her organizational heart might suck it right in. It just depends on her mood. I wait. SCDB-24 is swirling around her. She takes a breath and considers my idea.

The High Lord Regent loves organization as much as she

likes stuff, so I am speaking her native language. It's just a question of which nature will win. The season is right. The timing is right, but will she get the bug?

I step beside her. "Imagine a shelving unit that goes from here to here and to the ceiling," SCDB-24 is swirling everywhere now. "I think you could walk around this side of your car if all this stuff here were up on shelves here."

Then it happens. She sucks in the Spring Cleaning/Decluttering Bug. That's it. I've won. I hide my jubilation though I have been angling for this all year. Once my Honey gets the bug, radical amounts of stuff are allowed out of the house. Imagine if I had to make a dump run. A whole minivan full of stuff is gone. Oh, that sounds miraculous, but it could happen if she gets the bug bad.

"I'll need to buy a skill saw to make the shelves," I mention.

She borrows one from a friend within twenty-four hours and notifies me that I will be building the new garage shelving unit on Monday and it should be finished before we leave on vacation in a week. "I can do that," I reply.

Yes, she got SCDB-24 bad, really bad. If this mind virus were contagious, there would be a global pandemic and the municipal dumps would fill overnight. I took a van load of trash to the transfer station, built an excellent storage solution, ripped out two coat racks, and threw away stuff I didn't even know we still had. All before the vacation deadline. It was a win-win for me. Not only was I allowed to fix a clutter problem that had been irritating me for years, but The Lord Regent loves to see me working hard on projects so that is extra brownie points for me if you catch my drift.

I'M TOO EMBARRASSED

F ly check!" whispered one of the seniors just before we walked on stage. I verified that the zipper of my tux pants was indeed up. Being the guy with his barn door open during the whole performance was my literal nightmare.

If it had ever happened to me, I would still be having reoccurring nightmares about it twenty-five years later. That's how embarrassment works in my mind. It amplifies in the echo chamber of my skull and only ever dies out temporarily. Seven or fifteen years later, I will remember the event, and the feelings replay in my mind. None of the horror diminishes with time.

How about a bat in the cave? Have you ever had a booger caught in the nose hairs when you were taking wedding photos or during an important meeting? For me, when I'm in front of a classroom of students? My wife has a little mirror on the garage wall by her purse, and another at the top of the stairs, and another in the closet, and by her bed and in the bathrooms. It occurs to me now that I ought to use one of them for a 'bat check' before leaving the house for class.

One memory that won't die occurred after I sang a solo in front of my church for the first time. It went so well that everyone was clapping before the end of the song. I couldn't hear the track. I mumbled something silly, self-conscious, and stupid to explain what nobody had noticed, that I had stopped before the end of the song. Oh, my skin crawls with embarrassment even now. Why couldn't I have kept my mouth shut, walked off stage, sat down, and whispered my comment to my brother? Why did I speak it into the microphone and totally torpedo the song? Even all these years later, the embarrassment is too much for me. I've got to change the subject.

Some years ago, a former student contacted me online during my first attempt at tolerating the insanity of social media. She asked if I remembered her. I said that I did and asked how she was doing. She asked if I remembered that time when I farted in the middle of class? All the memories flashed back. In my first year of teaching, about the time when I learned that earning a four-year teaching credential had taught me nothing of value for a classroom, I was struggling to get the class to listen. If I recall, we were going through a spelling list. They were not cooperating. I belted, "WILL YOU ALL JUST BE QUIET," with my diaphragm fully engaged like a good singer should, and blasted a toot that reverberated over the noise of their chatter. That got their attention. They laughed and laughed and laughed. I gave up on spelling.

Embarrassment is a strange sort of terror. Why is it so

strong? It's like that cat pee smell that never really comes out of the back of your car after you left the window down that one night. Or the fishy smell that clings to your jeans after a weekend of dip netting on the Kasilof River. Even the memory of the worst of my physical pain, and there has been a lot of that, isn't as long-lived as embarrassment. Is it just me?

Oh. No. What if I'm the only one who feels this way? Now, that's embarrassing. I duck my head in shame and blink awkwardly. I imagine a world where I didn't just write six hundred words oversharing about boogers, farts, and my other embarrassing moments.

3D PRINTED HAPPINESS

The microwave oven transformed my expectations for how long it should take to have hot food on my plate. Slow cooking may taste better, but it taaaakes toooo looong!

The commercial air travel industry drastically adjusted the time and cost of traveling around the globe. If we still had to spend months getting to our tropical beach vacations, would they be vacations or voyages? Perhaps a once-in-lifetime adventure, but not a vacation. The risk of death is too high.

In my lifetime, computers had a similar effect on our expectations for information transfer. If what I need to know isn't on my screen in seconds, I get impatient. Not only do I expect the entire catalog of human knowledge and achievement in my pocket, but I require it to appear instantly when I want it.

Imagining thousands of years back, I suppose the invention

of the wheel had similar effects on ancient humans' view of manual labor. "Are you trying to tell me that I have to CARRY that slab of mastodon meat all the way back to camp? I'm not a caveman."

We are all the same, today's miracle is tomorrow's expectation. Give me what I want, when I want it, and how I want it. And faster.

3D printers are an interesting development in technology. Pop a design into a replicator machine and in three clicks, the real object appears. Okay! We aren't there yet, but 3D printing is revolutionizing many aspects of our world. My 3D printer uses plastic filament and prints a fragile version of my design, but the technology is being used to print rockets, meat, machine parts, and art in many different materials. I am not an expert, more of an enthusiast of the tool, but I think individualized manufacturing is amazing.

But I think it's time for something new and exciting.

Who is working on 3D printing happiness? Life is filled with difficulty, sadness, boredom, confusion, delay, and brokenness. I am sick of waiting. I want to be happy at the push of a button, and that button shall be forest green because I like that color best of all.

The concept sounds appealing. You could go online and find a design for happiness that meshes with your mood and send it to your desktop happiness printer. Bing! Bang! Boom! It goes to work laying down layer upon layer of good feelings in precisely the correct configuration while you get ready for your day and eat your bowl of Cinamon Toast Crunch. (Ah!

Happiness in a Bowl.)

When you pull the completed 3D-printed daily dose of happiness off the printer bed, you immediately feel great. No matter what the day has in store, you will have a happy day now. What a relief! How did the cavemen manage without this?

Many products have promised to make you happy in the past, but they've all failed to supply what you need. Lasting, genuine happiness. Most of them also have nasty side effects like ruining your health, your bank account, your peace of mind, your relationships, or your life in general. That is because they've all leaned their ladders against the wrong tree. The ME ME ME tree. You can't find lasting happiness there. That tree only grows "fleeting moments of happiness followed by deep disappointment" apples. The more you eat, the more you feel used, abused, and jaded. What if you climb higher and get the bigger apples at the top? Nope. They all taste the same, with that bitter aftertaste. Do you feel like a doofus? You've been gorging the wrong fruit this whole time. Don't worry, I've got a solution for you.

I've put a nice list together, which I think will serve you better than all the other stuff you've been trying. But first, let's redefine our goal. Happiness is not good enough. It's a bit of fluff floating in the wind. It's the wrong tree. Let's aim for Happiness's more resilient cousins. Contentment and Joy. They are genuine articles. Stable. Lasting. Pure. Get some of their fruit in your belly and life is going to improve from day one. So, now. To the list of how to 3D print Joy and Contentment each day.

1) Align your life with reality.

2) Live for something greater than yourself.

3) Make something.

4) Help People.

5) Spend time with someone important to you.

6) Share your heart.

7) Rest.

8) Repeat tomorrow.

HELICOPTER SEEDS: CREATIVITY

Three squirrels found my spruce tree in February. I watched them scurry through the branches devouring the seeds from a bumper crop of cones, a 'mast year.' They navigated out to the end of the branches with the grace of dancers, ripping the cones open to get at the seeds, all a frenzy. Spruce cone scales scattered under the buzzsaw of the harvesting teeth. Pieces rained down onto the snow below.

For some reason, the hyper reapers tended to fumble the cones after eating a few seeds. I'm not sure if they intended to do this, but it looked accidental. They would frantically move to tear the next one from the tree with the energy of a starving man at the buffet. Nibble. Nibble. Fumble. The snow below turned brown with detritus. Since the spruce tree is just outside my window I enjoyed their work from only a few feet away.

After the snow had melted enough in the spring to open

my garden gate, I saw that my gravel path was littered with cones and I remembered the hungry hunters of many months ago. I knelt and tossed a cone between my garden rows to compost. A shower of helicopter seeds streamed out in every direction. It felt like a magic trick. I found another cone and shook it to dislodge more seeds. The way that they whirred around with such elegance delighted me.

I was transported to a childhood memory. The giant cedar tree in our front yard once showered me with thousands of helicopter seeds when the wind hit its crown while I stood in our driveway. The seeds whirled down from a hundred feet in the air looking like very confused rain. I looked up for ten minutes or more, mesmerized by the display. I had never seen the cedar shed its seed before, much less been engulfed by it. It was utterly magical. When the shower ended, I scooped up handfuls of seeds and relaunched them for an hour.

Back in my garden, and forty-six years old again, I thought to grab a bag and collect some spruce seed. Perhaps I could grow some and sell seedlings. I planted some out under my hydroponic system lights and they germinated well. Not sure if I really have the space for spruce trees in my garden, but it is always interesting to experiment.

Now, in summer I find the spruce seedlings scattered everywhere. So many seeds were eaten, so many seeds were bagged by the gardener, so many seeds fell on the gravel path where there is no soil, and yet still other seeds fell in fertile soil and sprang up in their season.

As a creative, as an entrepreneur, as a parent, and as a thinker I can't help but see the object lesson in that. How much of the seed I produce every year fails to find fertile soil? How much of my work never germinates? Is it still worthwhile to make more seed, when so much is lost? Maybe I should give up and embrace the nihilistic point of view. Nothing matters. It's all pointless and useless in the end.

Then, just when I feel like giving up, a few of my seeds land soundly in fertile ground. They germinate and grow, stretching their tiny needle leaves toward the light. It's like a magic trick. My heart softens. Hopelessness is driven back like darkness from a struck match. All the work becomes worthwhile. All the early mornings become well utilized. All the long days transform with purpose. All the sacrifice becomes noble, a price I would pay again and again.

If only a few of my many toils produce a good result for the future, then how can I do anything but produce more seeds? As much as I can, for that is the only path to producing more seedlings. How can I do anything but scatter my creativity into the wind and hope that some of my work lands, lives, grows, and flourishes?

SUGAR ADDICTION: HAPPY CARB TUESDAY

It's another lovely Tuesday morning. The sun is shining and the sugar is flowing. On Carb Tuesday, you don't have to eat your vegetables first. You don't have to eat according to the dictates of body health and longevity. There is no need to exclude anything and protein is optional.

It feels like heaven for about three hours. Of course, then my body will be so overloaded that I'll need a mid-morning nap. My gut will be thrown for a loop de loop so extreme that Tuesday has become known for two things in my household. "Carbs, carbs, the musical fruit. The more you eat the more you--" Freeze frame.

Let me give you the back story. I've been intermittent fasting in earnest for four years now. I eat during a window between 5 am and 9 am and then I'm done for the day. Tuesdays are my cheat day. This program has helped me to gain some self-control in the food department. It is a foundational habit that I intend to keep in place permanently. I'm not interested in diets, I want a permanent life change. So I focus on making small changes in my diet, which can be sustained and stacked.

The fasting window helped me to understand the difference between what the body needs and what the brain wants. When it comes to food, my body needs X, but it craves Y, and Y is as much as I can stuff down my gullet. How great is the lesson that hunger is not an emergency? If only I had learned that thirty years ago.

As positive as Intermittent Fasting has been, about six months ago, I pulled out a new pair of pants, which had fit when I bought them but were now too tight. I'd gained some weight back! I don't do scales, so this was a shock to me.

"What?" I shrieked. "I've been good. I've been keeping my diet." Had my body turned against me or had I discovered a method of packing too many calories into my eating window? Probably both. My body had adapted to the restriction, maximized efficiency, and found a way to create a surplus which it could stack into my fat cells.

"Come on body. Help me help you." My body hadn't seen Jerry McGuire and didn't care about my hard work. I was getting fatter again. My blood filled with fury.

I shook my fist at the refrigerator. "You have betrayed me, Oh temptress. You fiend."

The same diet that had achieved steady, slow weight loss for years was now allowing gains? Come on! This felt utterly unacceptable. Time to get crazy or in the immortal worlds of Batman. "Now you wanna get nuts? Come on! Let's get nuts."

No carbs for you, body. See how you like them apples.

The next day, I stacked a no-carb rule on top of my four-hour eating window. I am usually a little overdramatic but I was miffed so I didn't let myself think about it. And I didn't tell anyone because I knew I would probably fail.

Day One: I noticed my brain accept the delicious cheesy meatballs with pepper sauce, look around my plate, and say, "That certainly tasted nice, but where is MY PRECIOUS?" That's right, carbs. My precious. Did you know that the greatest contribution The Lord of the Rings gave to society is in the best metaphor of addiction ever created? Gollum and the one ring.

Carbs had become my precious and my brain wanted its fix. How long had I been like this without realizing it? I considered this for several days. Well, how long have I been eating carbs? Could it be that I had been hooked on sugar my entire life?

My body complained and whined. It trembled and obsessed. My brain rationalized and manipulated just like a sidewalk junkie looking to score his next hit of Racehorse Charlie. What in the world was happening to me?

I survived day one and determined to push into uncharted territory. Day two. Was I getting the shakes? It's like a bad joke. Day three. I can't believe I'm still alive, frankly. Day four. Five. Six.

Then...Tuesday. Sweet Tuesday, my beloved friend. I will feast on carbs until sundown.

I remember taking the first bit of a cookie on that first Carb Tuesday. My head swam with the rush of it. I could feel pulsing energy behind my eyes, ringing in my skull. I knew at that moment that I was an addict. A sugar addict. And I knew that I needed to keep the No Carb + IF going for two reasons. My waistline and I needed to gain victory over this addiction.

Several months later, I have learned that I can do the unthinkable, difficult thing of living without carbs for six days a week. But Carb Tuesdays now get more anticipation and excitement than my birthday, so I'm pretty sure I haven't kicked my addiction yet.

I raise my fist at the refrigerator, "Oh temptress. You fiend."

YOU BIG BANG CHANG

Have you ever had that sinking feeling when you are rhyming gibberish words and accidentally cuss?

If I remember correctly, I learned my lesson in this regard on the playground in grade school. At the risk of recycling a fade, I'll demonstrate. "Hey, there's Jenny." You run over to Jenny and sing at the top of your lungs, "Jenny Jenny Bo Benny Banana Fanna Fo Fenny Fe Fi Fo Fenny Jenny!" Jenny either loves the song and joins in the chorus or hates it and tells you to stop. "Hey, there's Laurel." A group forms and runs over to Laurel and sings at the top of their lungs, "Laurel Laurel Bo Boral Banana Fanna Fo Faurel Fe Fi Fo Faurel Laurel!" What a delightfully fun and social game, I think. "Hey Ben, want to play the name game?"

"I guess so," I am hesitant to join in, but it looks like great fun. As soon as I agree someone in the group suggests, "Hey Ben, sing it for Chuck."

"Okay, sure," and in my best little boy soprano, I belt out. "Chuck, Chuck Bo Buck Banana Fanna Fo--" And another F-bomb is born. How lovely. The teacher probably overhears, if my luck holds.

It is amazing the life lessons you can learn at school. One: Chuck is on the dangerous names list in the name song game, but he's not alone. Two: If you're not ahead of the group, you're way behind. Three: Rhyming gibberish words are great fun.

I've taken great pleasure in using rhyming gibberish with my children, though not that song. I've learned that most moments are good times for surprising gobbledygook jingles, obnoxious puns, delightful nonsense phrases, and the like. They don't need to be amazing jokes because the bar is low in the category labeled Dad Jokes. Anything I say with a silly face cracks them up. Tip of the Day: Little kids think everything that is meant to be funny, is hilarious. It's great but beware. Just because your kids laugh at your jokes doesn't mean you're actually funny.

One of my daughter's favorite word salad games is when we accused each other with increasing volume and silliness, "Ya Big Bang Chang!" I think we are calling each other goofballs, but I'm not positive.

"No, you're a Big Bang Chang!"

It usually ends in a silly-face stare down and you know those can get pretty crazy.

After nearly a year of playing this game, it occurred to me that Big Bang Chang might have been coined by someone else. I flashed back to my rough playground days and the important lessons I learned there. What if I was teaching my kids an inappropriate phrase and didn't know it?

Let's check a few online dictionaries.

Big means "of considerable size, extent, intensity or seriousness." Okay, not bad. But if I tell my wife she looks "big" in that dress, I think that's a bad thing. "No Honey, you never look "big" in anything you wear."

How about Bang? "To (cause something to) make a sudden very loud noise or noises." Great, that one seems just fine. Wait. I scroll down further and read that it is a vulgar term for—what? Really?

Well, at least Chang doesn't mean anything. It's just pure gibberish. Nope, I'm wrong again. Chang means, "a large natural stream of water (larger than a creek).

In the urban dictionary, Chang Bang means, "to cry and whine like a manchild when a certain thing does not go your way."

Bang Bang means, "having a sudden, forceful, or attention-grabbing effect."

Stop the insanity! Can't a father just make up gibberish phrases to tease his daughter anymore? I'm putting my foot down. From this day forth. "Ya Big Bang Chang" means, "to accuse another person of being a silly, goofball." And I declare that there is no double meaning, bad meaning, twisted meaning, and it's not an urban dictionary insult. It's my new phrase, so I get to decide. Let the record also state that the phrase is derived from my daughter Johanna, who is the world's biggest Bang Chang and I love her to death for it.

LAMBORGHINI: VERSACE

I've got Lamborghinis coming out of my ears. Masaratis too. My garage is overflowing with monster trucks, race cars, and the like. As the valley girls of yesteryear would say, "I'm like so over it!"

I've got more dresses than I know what to do with. I've got Belle, Ariel, the Frozen Girls, Aurora, and the Sleeping Chick, or is that the same princess? I don't know...the dresses are different. So lovely. We must be prepared for every occasion. An evening stroll on the veranda or a royal ball. I've got more gowns than you can shake a stick at. I do love that expression, don't you?

I've got at least three complete tea sets, as one does. One for fancy occasions. "Bon Appetite." One for picnics in the park. "What a lovely time I am having." And one for when I feel like, forgive me, "slumming it." Don't worry if you clink the cups together too hard. They're only fake Versace.

I've got the summer house with the pool, the ski resort and the yacht. "Don't get me started, am I right?" The bungalow. The Safari house. The Hampton Mansion. A beautiful shorehouse at the cape. I've got the resort and the London flat. And then there's the penthouse in New York. "Sometimes I simply must fly in to catch a Broadway show. We don't dwell in caves, after all." But, they're all a bit of a bore. What I really need is a rustic hunting lodge, so I can rough it for a while. "Get my hands dirty, do you know what I mean? No, not literally. You're so funny!"

I've got the live-in chef, dining around the clock. The driver will take you where ever might be required, at any time of day. Take the Lamborghini if you like. It's the least we civilized folk require. Oh. The maids as well, because... well, you understand. "Good help is so hard to find, don't you think?"

Yes, I do have gardens, but let's not talk about them. They're not Chateau Versailles, if you know what I mean. Doesn't matter, I'm not outdoorsy anyway. I can't stand gardeners with all that dirt under their fingernails.

I've got the helicopter and the jet. "Oh, did I mention that already? My mistake."

***

Kids these days. They've got it made. How did we collect all these toys?

"Surely there is something we could get rid of?" I ask my wife. "The broken barbies. The Polly Pockets with no heads. The yacht with the snapped hinge. How about some of these plush pillows? Squishmallows. Is that really what they are called? Why do we have forty thousand of them? I think we could downside the model sports car collection. Aren't they just gathering dust? I know the Amazonian Gazebo cost a lot of money, but it also takes up four square feet of the house. That's one percent of the whole house, for an American Girl Gazebo. I'm not trying to be unreasonable, but do we really need ALL this stuff?"

My wife gives me a withering look. "You just don't understand."

I shrug. I definitely do not. "In my day, we were lucky to have sticks to play army man with."

Eyeroll.

I shrug again. "You can't win them all, I guess."

My wife smiles and bats her eyes like a Disney princess. "Honey Bear? Snook Ems? My Peanut Butter Pie?"

"Yes Dear?"

"The bathroom trash is getting full. Love you!"

GOLDEN THUMBS UP: HOT CARS

My father and I were sitting in a hot car with the windows rolled down. We had found a bit of shade, as I recall. The AC didn't work so the best you could hope for was a cross breeze and we were listening to Rush Limbaugh. The commercials came on. My Dad punched with the knuckle of his middle finger, seemingly without looking, and tapped off the power. We started talking. I don't remember how we started. My "talking in the hot car with Dad" memory is a composite of a thousand similar times, and that knuckle tapping the power knob probably happened a million times.

We always talked through the commercials. He had an extrasensory perception of when they would be ending. His fist would punch out toward the dash and knuckle tap Rush back on. The conversation ended until the next break.

Sometimes our conversation got really interesting and he would forget to tap back into Rush. It just depended if we were chitchatting or life chatting.

I remember the times when he would say he was proud of me and I would swell up like a balloon. I remember the times he would challenge me to be a better person, and I would sober up. I remember the times when we would laugh until we cried, and the times we would process through rancid circumstances. I remember when he would answer my endless questions. I remember the times when we would sit in silence and just hang together. Time with my Dad in the hot car, no matter what the conversation topic, was like a giant, golden Thumbs-Up Trophy.

I was a person of significance in the front passenger seat of that old car. He enjoyed hanging out with me and talking about big things with me. As a quality-time guy, I couldn't have custom-ordered a better affirmation. The Golden Thumbs Up.

I think our high calling, all of us, is to pass out these intangible encouragements to those beneath us on the ladder of life. When we treat a kid as a person of significance, they stand up straighter. When we notice a job they've done well, they are empowered to grow in competence. When we think they are important, they learn the truth. They are. The Golden Thumbs Up is a precious gift to the younger but only costs the older a little time and attention.

I remember every time I sat in that hot car with Dad and he casually pulled a Golden Thumbs Up from his pocket and dropped it in my lap. I snatched it up and treasured it. Still do. How precious is the work of the builder of hearts and the cultivator of minds? The parent. The teacher. The mentor.

The friend.

THE GUTTER TREE: GRIT

Outside my window is another townhouse, identical to mine. To my left, there are a dozen more, and to my right, the same. Cookie-cutter houses, all forty zero-lot lines are packed into an acre of land in the most economical arrangement.

As a man who yearns for the isolation of the woods, this is like a bit of grit stuck between my teeth. Not unlike how the oyster must feel when a grain of sand gets lodged between its mantle and its shell. It constantly irritates me.

To solve this in the back yard I have grown two trees to block the dozen condos on that side. It took twenty years to get them tall enough, but they are performing beautifully now. If I never focus past the trees, do those other structures exist? It's an existential-type question.

A solution is not possible in the front of my house. I have no dirt to plant a tree and no way to improve the view. So, I try to look up above the rooflines to the cottonwood trees that tower on the edge of our condo association. It's an imperfect solution, but circumstances are what they are. No point getting into them here.

In the gutter of my neighbor's house, a most interesting saga is playing out. I check in on it each day. A cottonwood tree has germinated in the gutter, subsisting on whatever dust has washed off the roof. It is pummeled by wind and weather. Twenty inches of snow and ice bury it for seven months, and then the summer comes and it pushes out a few leaves, reaches for the sun, and struggles to grow another half inch.

I can't help but root for the tenacious little tree. What grit under unreasonably limiting circumstances, what resilience, what patience. It is living the adage, "bloom where you are planted," so perfectly that I am humbled. How big would the tree be today if it had found deep soil instead of a rain gutter? Well, I don't have to wonder. One of the line of towering cottonwoods on the far side of the condo association is probably the parent of the gutter tree. Genetically, it is the gutter tree's destiny. But the gutter tree will never reach its potential.

Without soil to root deep into, the best the gutter tree can hope for is to cling to life on the sharp edge of reality until the inevitable happens. My neighbor cleans his gutters. Then he will be cast out of his hostile home and die in a white, plastic trash bag alongside broken egg shells and cantaloupe rind.

Unless I look out my window on that day. I will cross the drive and rescue the gutter tree. Perhaps I can find a wide, grassy meadow to plant its roots into. Then I can watch the gutter tree grow according to its potential at last. Perhaps the gutter tree will someday tower over my little cabin in the woods. Ravens and Magpies will rest in its branches. In July, someday far in the future, the gutter tree might scatter a million of its cotton-fluff seeds into the wind, and its line of tough-as-nail cottonwood trees will continue long after I have died.

WHAT IFs: GAME TIME

As I write this, I just finished teaching the first of three days in the inaugural Maker U summer camp. The schedule consists of twelve hands-on science projects and activities for kids, and I am relieved to report that it's going VERY well, though differently than I envisioned.

I've been stressing over whether each lesson and activity would succeed for so long that it's a genuine relief to have the event in motion. Will the kids understand this idea? Will they be enthusiastic about this thing that I think is fun and interesting? Did I get the age range and ability range correct? In the pregame phase of any endeavor, all you have is guesses, hopes, dreams, and a gut full of nerves.

I think I burnt too much energy in anxious anticipation of the event. Not that it didn't need planning, but it didn't need stressing over. Now that Maker U is rolling, I am awash with a flood of relief. Real-life data is pouring in. Some things are working. Other things are not and need to change. How beautiful to know. The game is on. The answers are finally here. Love that one! Some events are better than I thought they would be like dipping paper boats in wax to waterproof them. Other things don't make sense. They have too many steps, overcomplicated explanations, or they have poorly designed scorecards. So I call an audible and bury them as we go along. I change the plan to improve the kids' experience in the moment. I don't have to worry about "if" anymore. I just have to play the game.

I suppose this is similar to many other pieces of life. Finishing High School. Going on vacation. A first job, a new job. A big project. Having kids. Playing sports. Getting married. Oh, boy...now that I think about it, it's the same for every aspect of life. The pressure builds up in the planning and preparation and waits and builds and waits. Is it going to be a disaster? Why did I get myself into this? Will everyone think I am crazy? What if! What if? What—Boom!

It's time and all the pressure releases like an InstaPot blowing steam after a cook cycle. The mind focused on each moment and the playbook. Adrenaline pumps through your veins. And you do it. And you know the answers. And you can't worry anymore because you're too busy playing the game. Win or lose, it's a beautiful thing to play the game of life. To try something daring. To do something new. To experience something hard. To score points. To scramble and battle. To put all your preparation to use. To make something happen. That's what Maker U is all about. Be a maker, not a taker. Make something with your life. Don't just spend your days taking and taking and taking. Anyway...I've got to go.

I've got two more days on tap...no time to consider what if's, what about's, will they's, or I'm scared's. Real life is happening. Time to play the game.

BIG HAT NO CATTLE: BIG PENCIL NO LEAD

Have you heard the Texan insult, "Big hat, no cattle?" It's about integrity, having your words align with your lifestyle. If you talk and dress Big Cowboy, you should have a least one cow to back it up. I doubt that many do, but I've never lived in Texas. Perhaps every cowboy hat-wearing person has a few head of cattle behind their condo.

I grew up a California mountain boy and there was a country boy, redneck culture and uniform. It was not quite cowboy but definitely country music. Instead of a cowboy hat, it was a worn, sweat-stained baseball hat. If you lived the lifestyle salt crusted up the edge of the stain when the hat dried out. My baseball coach comes to mind. My childhood friend as well. They had animals, and land, and worked hard bucking hay. Though I did work for a summer on a homestead doing a little of that kind of work, I never really earned my sweaty hat. One time I stacked hay bales to the roof of a pole barn only to have the entire stack tip over and nearly bury me.

I transplanted to Alaska at the age of twenty-two and quickly noticed who the real Alaskan men and women were. Big fisherman. Big Hunters. A cabin in the wilderness. Cold hardened, icicles in the beard, dog mushing, trailblazing tough. Dall sheep hunting. "We don't change our plans for the weather, we change our clothes." Mountain climbing, mosquito-eating, river-boating, the last frontier is my playground, moose-meat freezer filling, real adventuring, Alaskan tough men and women. Oh yes. We're bigger than Texas, but you won't hear us bragging because we're surrounded by a million square miles of uncut wilderness that's so gorgeous it'll knock your head back. I mean, the sound literally will not travel that far. Alaskans don't feel the need to brag about our toughness. We're living in the American equivalent of Siberia by choice. Our grit speaks for itself.

What do you think the Alaskan equivalent to big hat, no cattle would be? Big parka, no snow machine. Or big net, no fish. Or a big ATV, no rifle. Big skis, no million-dollar mountain vista selfies. Big boat, no halibut. Big shovel, no snow. Big tires, no studs. Big plans, no homestead. Shoot! The last one is me. Maybe I'll have to work on that. Am I a real Alaskan after twenty-something years? Not sure, but I do live here. Doesn't that say something? Maybe it says that I'm a little bit crazy. Alaska crazy. I don't recall ever hearing an Alaskan boast like a Texans do. Alaskans are a different breed of tough. I'm not sure where I fit into it all as a writer and teacher. Big pencil, no lead. Oh no! Now I can't stop.

I suppose you have a version of big hat, no cattle where

you live. What do you call people who don't live up to the stereotypical norm in your area? They talk big but lack the substance.

As I mount my little electric peddle-assisted bicycle and take on mile after mile of Alaska wilderness trail by my house, I figure that it's fine to not be quite as tough as my Alaska neighbors. I won't talk large and posture big, not without having the receipts. The real substance I'm after is character, skill, and integrity. Skip the bluster and show. How should we reframe this for modern times? I got it. I don't want to be "all Instagram, no real life." That's most of our problem these days, social media fakery.

Better to let who we are and what we do speak for itself. As a writer and a teacher, I should strive to be "short pencil, lead well spread" rather than "big pencil, no lead."

PERFECTION?

There is nothing more dangerous to a writer than perfection. Approaching a blank page as if an illusive set of words, containing no flaws, exists and waits for the mind to conceive them so they can grace the page with their splendor. It's a fool's errand. Expecting perfection constipates your word factory. I mean completely shuts it down. Why do I fall into thinking I can produce greatness on command?

"No problem. Perfection on 3. Ready? 1,2, "Fart." Yah. That's about right.

I've come to believe I shouldn't concern myself with perfection. It's the pot of gold at the end of the keyboard. It's the fantasy that I sell myself when I think my life needs to proceed like a blockbuster movie. Blah!

How could I get anything down on paper if my standards are so high? What if I don't reach perfection? Then what?

I failed. No! I can't live up to those expectations. I'm just a writer, a humble...an ordinary writer.

That doesn't mean my mind doesn't create spectacular third acts for everything I do.

An ordinary writer surprises his wife...no shocks everyone, by writing an international bestseller, a cultural icon, an instant classic...No!... a world-changing..." The gears of reality grind like the manual transmission on the first day of driver's ed class.

What if this book is so good and someone important notices it, they make a movie out of it, and the story becomes a bestseller, and I end up rich and famous? All because I wrote this perfect sentence! Meanwhile, the cursor blinks idly on a blank page.

I slap my metaphorical cheek. Wham!

"Snap out of it, Ben."

I get a drink of water.

"Stop living in LaLaLand."

"But I like it there," I whine.

"There is no there THERE. It's pure fantasy."

"But what if?"

"Shut up, Ben!" I chide myself. "Do some work."

Am I the only one who gets whipped around the whirlpools

of dreams not meeting reality? That miserable sucking sound is your life satisfaction and work productivity spinning ever deeper into the drink.

"All I'm hoping for is perfection and greatness. IS THAT TOO MUCH TO ASK FOR?"

It's probably a little different for you. What version of perfection are you dreaming of? Money? Respect? Do you want to be beautiful? Funny? Successful? Intelligent? You want a better fill-in-the-blank? I know! You want to tell the world what to do, when to do it, and it would be nice if they would say thank you once in a while. Are you frustrated because the world keeps resisting your dictatorship? I know, it's hard. You keep thinking that you deserve it. After all, you've suffered. You've been patient. You can supply all the requisite rationalizations, it's what you're best at.

Give yourself a metaphorical SLAP on the cheek with me today. Life is not going to be perfect. Stop expecting everything to be just right.

"Without my dreams, I've got NOTHING!"

That's a little overdramatic! I like it. Let's consider the question.

As a writer, I should try to be honest. I should improve my craft from project to project. I should be diligent over time. I should savor the joy of putting ideas and stories down on paper. I should think of myself as an ordinary, humble, happy writer. I should just do the work.

"But I've got no prestige, no influence, no yacht..."

I should cultivate contentment in all circumstances for if I can not be happy with nothing, I will never be happy with wealth, power, and influence.

PERENNIALS: CHRONIC PAIN

I find it hard to talk about my chronic pain. Perhaps because it's always there, nothing has changed, and one coping mechanism is pretending it's fine. After thirty-six years, are updates required? Perennial pain is just a part of my life and will continue to be.

As I lay a foam kneeling pad in front of a freshly turned soil bed, I know that I will have to pay for planting out fifty asparagus seedlings. Pain is a cost of doing business with my body. It has been since I was a kid. The only question is will it hurt for one day or two weeks? As each fragile plant goes into fertile soil, I am careful with my body ergonomics to try to minimize the price of admission, but I can feel the strain in the back. In the knees. My muscles tremble with the strain of stabilizing joints that lack their natural integrity. These seedlings are so small. I wonder if I should have grown them up under the lights longer, or if they may as well transition into the real world since the temperatures aren't getting below forty degrees anymore. What do I know about gardening?

I do know I hate chronic pain. It's like beach sand sprinkled in an omelet. Its unpredictable, sickening crunch ruins the fluffiness of so many moments. Playing catch with my son. Dancing in the living room with my girls. Taking walks with my wife. Sand in the Craw teaches its lessons. I have learned to be slow and steady. Careful and thoughtful avoids the electric zinger down to the bone.

Pain is also like spilled paint, it marks everything it touches. Sometimes you get tired of finding discomfort's fingerprints all over the house. The carpet. The refrigerator. The bedspread? Really? If you aren't careful, you can track pain onto everything and everyone you love.

I've decided to evict chronic pain from my house and move it down the street to the junkie house on the corner. Living with pain is no way to live. Though pain likes to reinvade my mind like an unwelcome houseguest, I try to be strict and clear with it. Easier said than done. "Your words have no power here, chronic pain. You don't get to rule my emotions. You don't get to influence my words. You're not the boss of me!" What do I know about living with pain? Many folks have it worse than I do. That much is certainly true, but pain is not a contest. We all bear our share and that's that.

So, I keep a constant eye on mine. It's like there's a Wily Coyote, always trying to blow up my day. Didn't it seem that Road Runner took such pleasure in evading Wily Coyote's schemes in those old cartoons? I can relate to that. When I have a good day, despite the pain, I feel quite gleeful. I've given Wily Coyote the slip. Ha! Ha!

Pain has taught me many things. Chief among them all is this. 2 Corinthians 12:9, "But he said to me, "My grace is sufficient for you, for my power is made perfect in weakness." Therefore I will boast all the more gladly about my weaknesses, so that Christ's power may rest on me. NIV

SPIDERMOOSE: GIANT PEANUT BUTTER CUPS

The giant beast approached, with all its horrific hairy legs. I counted eight like a tarantula, but they did not look arachnid. The mega-jointed legs had hooves and fur like a moose. I jolted in shock, but could not move away. The creature stepped to within striking distance. I craned my neck upward. Something had malfunctioned in my body. My mind reached for any muscle that remained under my command, but none existed. A moose's body, head, and antlers hovered at the center of its long legs. I stood paralyzed and at the mercy of the terrible SpiderMoose. "What are you?" I managed to blurt.

"I'm completely your fault. That's what I am," replied the Moose. Its voice sounded like a Muppets character which gave me some relief. You can tell a lot from monster voices in movies, you know.

"My fault? How can that be?"

"You ate too close to bedtime. That giant peanut butter cup, remember?" The SpiderMoose's teeth clacked with each word.

"Oh. That's right. I did, but it was so delicious. My daughter made them. They were magnificent."

"When will you learn that if you eat too close to bedtime you never sleep well?" The mighty SpiderMoose pulled back its lips in a disgusting approximation of a smile. It struck me as more grotesque than the melding of bug and mammal. My body filled with dread like a bucket with acid, sloshing and biting.

"Are you going to chew my head off now?" I trembled.

"It wouldn't be much of a nightmare if I didn't, now would I?" The SpiderMoose clamped its jaws over my face and-- I woke up in a cold sweat. The clock read 1:30 am.

Why do I do these things to myself? Sure the fear fades the moment I hear the comforting sounds of reality (In this case, an artificial waterfall soundmaker) and my wife shuffling around in the kitchen. Does she ever sleep? But seriously, why do I do this to myself? The menu may as well have read: A lovely, giant peanut butter cup with a doozy of an afterburner during the REM cycle.

As I lie awake in my sweat-soaked bed, I wonder how many of my life's emergencies, tragedies, panics, and unfortunate events could have been avoided, if I had just given a few seconds of thought beforehand. Don't believe me? Just follow

"The Science!"

Car crashes: 95%, AVOIDABLE

Money trouble: 87- 94%, PREVENTABLE

Relational trouble: 78.5%, NOT A SURPRISE

Natural disasters: 79%, FORESEEABLE

Loneliness: 84%, SELF-INDUCED

Nightmares: 99%--Who am I kidding? I'm just plucking these numbers out of thin air.

But it makes me wonder, at 1:54 am, how much of the crap in life is self-induced nightmares. Are we victims of cruel fate? Or did we order another SpiderMoose off the menu along with that giant peanut butter cup?

THE POSTAGE STAMP: BLOOM IF YOU DARE

Three years ago, I enrolled in a plant propagation course. Not at a university. In my backyard. The professor is strict, often failing projects with only the meagerest of feedback. I receive a red, capital F circled aggressively six times in the form of dead plants, chewed plants, broken plants, or sun-starved plants. My thumbs are decidedly UNgreen at this point, but I'm hopeful for the future.

Gardening is a challenge in Alaska. Gardening in my backyard is doubly so. It is a postage stamp surrounded by townhouses. That means the light is sporadic at best and the winters are brutal.

For example, this winter the snow load stepped on my berry bushes like an elephant. Snapped, flattened, and demoralization is par for the course in my backyard. Most plants can't handle living under an ice cube for seven months straight. These berry bushes are tenacious though. They'll get back up and grow back stronger this summer. They better or they'll die. I am very little help. Maybe I'll get a few berries from them. There is nothing better than grazing berries in late summer. Then the snow will stomp them again and the mice will tunnel around my garden to strip their bark clean. The berry bushes will have to start from ground level next spring.

I feel all my plants staring at me when I sit in my backyard, "A little help would be nice," they seem to cry. But when I do something, it's usually wrong. Planted too early- the last snowstorm in May kills them. Planted too late- Fall comes before harvest. Planted in the wrong place- not enough light. In Alaska, the window for success is narrow. And that's if you start with the correct plant. I've learned to just throw everything into the garden to see what survives. It's a high-stakes game for the plants and I waste more money than I should. What can I say? Education is expensive these days. Have you heard how much university tuition has skyrocketed? My backyard college is a steal in comparison.

I tell myself, once I figure out this propagation thing, I'll be printing money. Every plant that I propagate is free forever. One plant becomes two. Two becomes four. Four becomes infinity, eventually. Right?

Of course, there are other outcomes like total failure and demoralization. In my backyard education, I've learned that total failure is temporary and demoralization lasts only a season. Then I, like my tenacious berry bushes, will pull myself up out of the mud and try again, unreasonably filled with hope for the future, armed with the knowledge of what didn't succeed, and brimming with new strategies to test.

DRIVE-BY SNIFFINGS: BAGEL VOYEURISM

It was late on the sixth day of my zero-carb week. In less than thirty minutes, I would be asleep, blissfully unaware of my empty belly. Best of all, tomorrow was my cheat day. Carbohydrate Day occurs on Tuesdays. It's basically a holiday. That Phil Wickham song that says, "Friday's good cause Sunday's coming," has been co-opted in my house to "Sunday's good cause Tuesday's coming!"

I clicked on a YouTube video about Utopia Bagel in New York City and something completely crazy happened. I uttered a set of words I've been avoiding my entire life, "I want to go to New York City." My wife looked up from her to-dos with a look of ecstasy. She's wanted to go forever. The greatest city in the world. The Big Apple. The words had barely exited my mouth when I realized I must be carb-starved-crazy. You see, I've spent most of my life being repulsed by New York City.

First of all, millions of people crammed into a small space mathematically equals a no-go zone. Mall or Manhattan.

No go. Second, I don't buy the New York sales pitch. When everyone says it's the greatest city in the world, they are reading off the same script. That's a red flag. How about an honest review? Like: Alaska. The bears will eat you. The mosquitoes will suck your blood. The wilderness kills, BUT it's gorgeous.

Am I evolving as a person? Hm. Perhaps it's just the carb restriction talking, but I would brave the millions of grumpy people in NY to try a fresh Utopia Bagel. On a Tuesday. It's on my list. Have you heard of Bucket Lists? I'm starting a New York Bagel List. Which we will now define as a list of things I'm willing to grudgingly endure to attain an undeniably positive end. I suppose that's what my no-carbohydrate diet is, enduring discomfort today to reach my health goals in the future.

Well, that's all for now. Until Tuesday, you can find me drive-by-sniffing other people's desserts, and scrolling YouTube for bagel voyeurism videos.

(If you would like to become a Bagel Voyeur, follow these steps. Eat zero carbohydrates for six days, then watch this video, https://youtu.be/mSuAcDiwkk4?si=x_KQIgAgFTphZZbH)

OTHER PEOPLE'S BALLOONS: INSULT THE COOK

Imagine a home-cooked meal set out on a life-worn table. A roasted chicken, mixed vegetables, and French bread. Probably a salad too. A family assembles around the steaming dishes. Dad thanks God for the meal and expresses gratitude "for the hands that prepared it."

That was every night for me growing up. Except my Dad was never satisfied with the ritual of asking God to bless the hands that prepared the food. He would stuff a massive bite of chicken in his mouth and savor the crispy skin and juicy breast meat. I remember him saying, "That is amazing, Honey!" or some derivation of that every night. Then he would take a bit of the mixed vegetables and declare, "Those vegetables are so perfectly seasoned." My mom buttered and oven-toasted her French bread. It was always golden brown and it melted in the mouth. He would chew with his eyes closed, total relish in his expression. "Oh! That's so good. It's like a culinary..." and then he would search for the right word. Melted butter glistened on his lip. "A culinary orgasm." Mom glowed with pride. Dad would kiss Mom.

At that point, we kids would realize that we should probably say something too. "Thanks for the food," we chorused. For us, it was food. For Dad, it was a culinary orgasm. It was many years later that I learned the usual usage of that word.

Maybe there are two kinds of people in the world. Those that express gratitude lavishly and the other kind. The ones that never miss an opportunity to insult the cook. "This seems a little overdone," or "Didn't I tell you that I prefer no salt on my omelet?" or "Next time, Honey...can you not cook such a big portion?" How about the non-verbal grunt of disapproval or the verbal processing complaint? "I asked for a bacon cheeseburger tonight, and I was looking forward to it all day. It got me through all the stress of the day BUT I guess teriyaki chicken is fine."

If all cooks had balloons for hearts, and they probably do, one of them just got popped. The contrast between the two is so stark. So blatant. It gives me pause. How do my words ripple from my mouth to other people's balloons? What if we could see the effects of our words so clearly? So instantly. Pop! Pop! Pop! Maybe our words have more power than we give them credit for. We can refill sagging balloons or pop them.

How much would our world improve if we ALL started practicing lavish gratitude?

GRADUATION: BIZZARO WORLD RAFTING TRIP

Graduation hats are weird. Who came up with the idea that to properly celebrate my child's graduation I had to glue a square piece of cardboard to the top of her head? "Oh, that's lovely, but how about a yellow tassel that will swing in front of her eye." It makes no sense to me. My wife and I bought two of those zany-looking hats this year. My oldest graduated high school and my youngest kindergarten.

That's right. I have one child making me feel old and another keeping me young. Scratch that. They both make me feel old but in different ways. With my oldest, I am brainstorming business plans, recommending accounting software, booking gigs, and teaching professional etiquette. How can I be old enough to have a child starting a career? When did that happen?

My youngest climbs up the stairs each morning with the craziest bed hair in the world and absolutely must snuggle with me on the couch until she fully wakes up...and play the little thumb people game...or the talking hand puppets game...or the 'rigid as a stick' gum game...or perhaps we'll invent something new this morning. She still needs help getting that over-tight sweater off and won't eat her oatmeal if it has too much cinnamon. My energy reserves never outlast her enthusiasm. I'm either getting old or feeling like it.

My life feels like a bizarro world rafting trip through the Grand Canyon where I am jumping between six different rafts, trying to keep my footing and steer the whole lot around the rocks. From driving lessons to toothbrushing. From Rubix cube competitions to dance recitals. From 'good morning' routines to 'night night' routines. From 'sticky-kisses' on ouches to brainstorming novel plots at Taco Bell.

Graduations are a great opportunity to pull the rafts onto the riverbank for a while, to slow down, and light a campfire. Just to reminisce. Look what we have accomplished together. Look what we have been through. To laugh and cry as a family and probably roast s'mores.

ABOUT THE AUTHOR

B.T. Higgins lives amongst the rugged beauty of Alaska's potholes, street lamps, cul-de-sacs, and townhouses with his wife and their four children, where they homeschool together and follow Jesus. A thinker, maker, and lifelong learner, he spends his days teaching, writing, and occasionally being a motivational couch potato. B.T. believes that the most meaningful thing he can do with his life is serve God and other people, though he secretly wishes he could do it all from a quiet spot in the woods with just his thoughts for company.

B.T. has a deep appreciation for humor, music, podcasts, and the wonder of nature. He draws inspiration from life's ordinary moments, seeing in them lessons worth preserving. His experiences as a husband, father, and observer of the human condition have taught him much, and he is thankful that while time slips through our fingers, wisdom can be collected, utilized, and shared.

He is the author of three nonfiction books for adults focused on family, parenting, and faith. He has also written several middle-grade fiction novels that explore the super cool questions constantly swirling in his head. Whether writing for kids or adults, B.T. Higgins hopes to inspire, challenge, and entertain—but not necessarily in that order.

ALSO BY B.T. HIGGINS

Adult Non-Fiction

Father and The Wolves

Fixing Education

Middle-Grade Fiction

Danielle and The Zero Gravity Suit

The Pocketeer

The Cracking of Monday Egg

The First Circle of Monday Egg

Minty Nothingmore: The House on Rocky Ridge

Raykin Smythe: The Last Red Ship

Minty Nothingmore: The Magician's Guild

Becoming the Plagarist

The Master of Disaster

FOLLOW B.T. HIGGINS

bthiggins.substack.com

B.T. Higgins

WWW.BTHIGGINS.COM

www.ingramcontent.com/pod-product-compliance
Lightning Source LLC
LaVergne TN
LVHW012247070526
838201LV00090B/140